Dramatizing the Content
With Curriculum
Readers Theatre

Rosalind M. Flynn

INTERNATIONAL
Reading Association
800 BARKSDALE ROAD, PO BOX 8139
NEWARK, DE 19714-8139, USA
www.reading.org

Executive Editor, Books	Corinne M. Mooney
Developmental Editor	Charlene M. Nichols
Developmental Editor	Tori Mello Bachman
Developmental Editor	Stacey Lynn Sharp
Editorial Production Manager	Shannon T. Fortner
Production Manager	Iona Muscella
Supervisor, Electronic Publishing	Anette Schuetz
Project Editor	Stacey Lynn Sharp

Cover Design, Linda Steere; Art, © JupiterImages Corp./clipart.com

Library of Congress Cataloging-in-Publication Data
Flynn, Rosalind M. Dramatizing the content with curriculum-based readers theatre, grades 6-12 / Rosalind M. Flynn.
    p. cm.
Includes bibliographical references and index.
1. Active learning. 2. Middle school education--Activity programs. 3. Education, Secondary--Activity programs. 4. Readers' theater. 5. Drama in education.
6. Teaching--Aids and devices. I. Title.
  LB1027.23.F59 2007
  371.39'9--dc22

ISBN-13: 978-1467921558
ISBN-10: 1467921556

To the Fam—Mal, Audra, Justine, and Timmy—for making your magnificent entrances and playing your parts so joyfully.

Here's to past and future dramatizing of the content that is our lives.

CONTENTS

ABOUT THE AUTHOR

 Rosalind M. Flynn is an educational drama consultant who conducts arts integration workshops and residencies with teachers, artists, and students in classrooms throughout the United States. She earned her Bachelor of Arts degree in Drama at The Catholic University of America in Washington, DC, where she is presently an adjunct professor in the same department. She completed both her master's degree in Education and her PhD in Curriculum and Instruction at the University of Maryland. Her doctoral research focus was the use of drama as a learning method.

Rosalind's five national touring workshops for teachers were developed in collaboration with the Education Department of The John F. Kennedy Center for the Performing Arts. One of those workshops, "Dramatizing the Content: Curriculum-Based Readers Theatre," is the foundation for the contents of this book. Since 1994, she has conducted workshops for students and teachers from 41 states and the District of Columbia. Her personal and professional goal is to bring that number of states up to 50 before her journey ends.

Rosalind has been a classroom teacher and a theater director with elementary, middle-level, high school, and college students. She is the coauthor of *A Dramatic Approach to Reading Comprehension* (Heinemann, 2006). For the Washington Performing Arts Society, in Washington, DC, she is the Youth Education Consultant—observing, consulting with, and leading professional development experiences for artists who perform and teach in schools. Rosalind hopes that this book encourages middle school and high school teachers to try a new instructional approach and experience Curriculum-Based Readers Theatre. She lives in Silver Spring, Maryland. You may contact Rosalind by e-mail at RMCFlynn@aol.com.

The college professor whom I respected most emphasized that nearly all people learn best by some form of "doing." When I began teaching high school theater and English, I fully embraced this belief. However, it didn't take me long to realize that while my theater classes were full of "doing"—students engaging and investing in active, dynamic classroom work—my English classes were not. Looking back now from a perspective of almost 30 years, I think that is where my work with Curriculum-Based Readers Theatre (CBRT) began.

My Journey in Developing CBRT

Act I

In my graduate studies, I began searching for ways to infuse the drama and theater I loved into other areas of the curriculum. Primary-age students are usually eager to participate in classroom dramatic activities, but students' enthusiastic willingness to take risks seems to diminish beyond about fifth grade. My goal, therefore, became to find accessible theater activities that would offer active classroom learning experiences to older students.

These drama or theater activities, I quickly realized, would have to be safe and purposeful enough for adolescents and teenagers to agree to participate in, to take risks, and to leave their chairs and try something different. The learning purposes of the activities would also have to be crystal clear to both the teachers and the students. Otherwise, no matter how absorbing or enjoyable the activities might be, their tenure in the classroom would be short-lived.

My search led me to a wealth of ideas for infusing drama into the curriculum—some ideas better than others, of course. I began working directly with classroom teachers and my challenge became to consider first the content area they were studying and then how I might address the learning objectives through drama. The idea for CBRT was conceived when I was faced with a social studies chapter full of facts and devoid of interesting characters or tension of any kind. How could I get students to dramatize the content of that chapter in a meaningful way in 45 minutes? Readers Theatre is what I latched onto, and that first social studies script inspired me to find ways to directly connect Readers Theatre to a wide variety of content areas.

There are numerous publications on Readers Theatre. Perform an Internet search for "Readers Theatre" and you will get lots of hits—many of them containing free downloadable scripts and many of them quite worthwhile. Most resources focus on story or literature-based scripts, and if you find a script that corresponds precisely with your classroom literature, the Readers Theatre lesson plan is practically complete. If, however, stories and literature are not the mainstay of the subject area being taught—as in the aforementioned social studies classroom—teachers will likely abandon any notions of Readers Theatre in the classroom. Some available resources contain scripted curriculum topics, but most of them are only narrowly applicable—in other words, only rarely will teachers come across a script that precisely addresses the content being taught.

In those cases where teachers do find pertinent scripts, other difficulties arise. Typically, these scripts feature speaking parts for a relatively small number of speakers—an average of only 4 to 10 speakers, not enough roles for full class involvement. In most classrooms I've worked in, students prefer having a speaking role in the script over listening to their classmates read the script aloud. Another occasional downside is that sometimes the speakers are assigned passages of dialogue far too long for them to deliver effectively. For example, I've seen scripts with speeches of 200-plus words for a solo speaker—far too lengthy, in my experience, for most student readers or performers and their audiences. In some instances, the script's language is stilted and unnatural for young speakers, containing phrases like "several deductions have been postulated" or "brimming with escapades and wanderlust." Few students read aloud so beautifully that their classmates enjoy and benefit from hearing them read a lengthy passage—especially if the language of the passage is complex.

My response to these difficulties was to have students write original scripts. Motivated by the work of commissioned playwrights hired by theaters to write scripts about specific topics, I reasoned that if playwrights could take pieces of information, historical episodes, or narratives and adapt them as scripts with lines of dialogue for a given number of characters, students and teachers could do something similar. I could help them take the contents of a textbook, a novel, or almost any collection of facts and script the information in creative ways. We could write the scripts so that every member of the class could have a solo speaking role.

Therefore, I conceptualized the formula for CBRT: Focus the scripts on the precise curriculum content being taught. Create a script with as many solo speaking parts as there are students in the classroom. Use language that is clear, concise, and maybe even contemporary. Involve students in the writing process and then give them the opportunity to perform the script.

Act II

In association with the Education Department of The John F. Kennedy Center for the Performing Arts, I developed a teacher workshop called "Dramatizing the Content: Curriculum-Based Readers Theatre." Because the Kennedy Center's professional development program has a national component, I have had the privilege of presenting this workshop all over the United States. Workshop presentations led to work in hundreds of classrooms where I have learned much more about the process of creating and performing CBRT.

The content of the CBRT scripts that my work has generated directly addresses prescribed standards of learning that teachers must teach and assess (see chapter 1 for more discussion). For that reason, middle school and high school teachers frequently request the CBRT workshop and residencies. With their students, I have developed CBRT scripts on topics as varied as types of triangles, improper fractions, dangling modifiers, Meso-America, women's suffrage, the scientific method, light and sound waves, elapsed time, and classification of organisms.

The Charles County Public Schools in Maryland, for example, created a CBRT residency for me in five of its middle schools in 2002. The project's 17 CBRT scripts were developed with students and teachers during four-day residencies at each participating school. The students, teachers, and I spent the residency sessions creating scripts that would accurately reflect curriculum content and entertain our audiences. We collaborated on a variety of scripts with topics that included novels, the Constitutional Convention, the elements of a story, theme, characterization, and nutrition.

In the Selma/Dallas County schools in Alabama during three extended visits in 2004, I worked with students and teachers from seven different schools in grades 1 through 9. The process began with teachers participating in my professional development workshop. Following the workshop, I visited each teacher's classroom on three separate occasions to develop, revise, and rehearse the original CBRT scripts. The script topics ranged from the nine planets to the mathematical order of operations to the Transcontinental Railroad. Our project culminated in a citywide "Readers Theatre Blitz" in which all seven classes assembled and appeared onstage to perform their original CBRT scripts.

In my work in 2003 and 2004 with high school students in Oklahoma City and Indianapolis, CBRT script topics included improper fractions, the water cycle, women's suffrage, Advanced Placement Spanish, how to draw the human face, and the parts of a cell. Between 2004 and 2006, I conducted residencies with students in the Washington, DC, Public Schools and developed scripts on topics like adjectives, fractions, the scientific method, the novels *Katie's Trunk* (Turner, 1997) and *The Phantom Tollbooth* (Juster, 1989), the 13 colonies, saturated solutions, figurative language, the southeast United States, and prefixes and suffixes.

In Wooster, Ohio, and Sarasota, Florida, my CBRT work with teachers and students has been the focus of research projects. The Ohio study validated the efficacy of CBRT for improving students' reading fluency and retention of science content information. The Sarasota study affirmed the value of CBRT in middle school classrooms for increasing student literacy and retention of information, and appealing to students with wide variations in academic ability.

Teachers repeatedly report CBRT victories like a student scoring 100 on a vocabulary test when he usually gets a 20 or 30, the whole class earning a B or above on the same American Revolution test that last year's class pretty much flunked, reluctant readers clamoring for more lines in a script, and students investing in the rehearsal and performance process. Students offer comments like "When I am performing a script I enjoy it and the information I am saying sticks in my head, so I am learning more than a teacher just telling me the information" or "Playing a part and interacting with the information gets the facts burned into your memory (in a fun way) and helps you *want* to remember."

My experiences make me think that the "theatre" in Readers Theatre has the potential to reclaim, in a small way, a piece of something that seems to have pretty much vanished from American schooling—the class play. I remember whole afternoons in sixth grade dedicated to rehearsing the class play. I remember going to middle school with a sense of purpose—preparing the performance and anticipating the audience who would soon enjoy all our hard work. I remember being allowed to present my book report as a script performed for my classmates instead of a report written in cursive on lined filler paper. I remember my 12th-grade English teacher approving my group's request to perform a version of Japanese Noh theater rather than write a paper and give an oral report on it. I also remember much of the content of those educational drama experiences, which, in addition to what I have witnessed in my work, strengthens my belief in the many learning purposes of CBRT.

Act III

The years spent presenting that workshop for teachers across the United States and conducting CBRT residencies with students have increased my understanding of how to write, read, rehearse, and present student-created scripts focused on curriculum information. I decided that I needed to make all that I have learned about CBRT more widely available—thus this book. The chapters in this book provide secondary school teachers with a framework for understanding, introducing, writing, revising, assessing, rehearsing, and performing CBRT with students in grades 6–12.

There may be more acts to come in my CBRT production. Teachers have shared stories about extending the process beyond the confines of curriculum and creating scripts about classroom procedures, anti-bullying, memories of the school year, manners, tolerance, and the importance of kindness. For now, my hope is that the contents of the chapters that follow inspire teachers of grades 6–12 to channel students' enthusiasm for creating and performing and add CBRT to their teaching repertoire.

Organization of This Book

The book's first chapter, "Understanding Curriculum-Based Readers Theatre," provides an introduction to CBRT, grounding its use in the disciplines of reading fluency, reading comprehension, and authentic arts integration. Chapter 2, "Beginning Curriculum-Based Readers Theatre," outlines how to introduce CBRT to students, providing all of the information teachers need when exposing students to CBRT for the first time. Chapter 3, "Collaborating With Students on an Original Script," instructs you how to work with students to write a collaborative model CBRT script. You will learn how to encourage students to make entertaining scripts by using an interesting context (a movie coming attraction, a TV commercial, a game show, for example), contemporary language, and humor, if appropriate, and to ensure that students accurately include the specified content information. You will also learn about working with students to read through and revise the collaborative model CBRT script.

After the students' first exposure to CBRT, they can use the process to create their own scripts. In chapter 4, "Involving Students in Independent Scriptwriting," you will learn to involve students in creating and assessing their own scripts. This chapter includes guidelines for independent student scriptwriting, a CBRT script assessment checklist, and instructions for small-group CBRT scriptwriting. Chapter 5, "Staging a Curriculum-Based Readers Theatre Performance," presents the "theatre" aspect of CBRT, explaining the value and processes of performance, including

- assigning solo speaking parts and rehearsing,
- coaching the students to prepare them as performers,
- presenting for an audience of any size—large or small, and
- assessing the student as CBRT performer.

You will also find three useful appendixes to support your implementation of CBRT. In Appendix A, you will find a variety of sample CBRT scripts spanning a range of topics and content areas, which you are encouraged to reproduce and use in your own classroom. You can also find sample scripts on my website at www.rosalindflynn.com. Appendix B provides script templates to aid you in creating scripts with your students. These templates are intended to simplify the script creation process for teachers and students who need additional support and ideas. Appendix C provides instructions on computer formatting CBRT scripts, breaking down the process in simple steps.

Throughout the text, I offer snapshots of moments from my own experiences with students and teachers in sections called "CBRT in Action." Theater terminology that appears in boldface type within the text is defined in nearby sidebars. To give readers a taste of the wide variety of topics and their creative treatments in CBRT script form, excerpts called "Script Sections" appear within the chapters as do selected complete CBRT scripts.

Acknowledgments

It appears that it takes a nation to write a book. My thanks, therefore, to the following supportive citizens and establishments:

- Barbara Shepherd in the Education Department of The John F. Kennedy Center for the Performing Arts, for making my professional development workshops part of the Partners in Education touring programs, and to her colleague Amy Duma for being a continual impetus to excellence.

- All the arts and education organizations around the United States that enhanced my understanding of this body of work by bringing me to work with their students and teachers. A special gesture communicating gratitude to the following: Marsha Carmichael, Sandy Greene, and Lisa Morenzoni in Alabama; Jim Carpenter in Maryland; Leslie Lacktman and Judy Hall in Florida; Jeannette Spencer McCune in Washington, DC; Ellen Westkaemper in South

Carolina; Debbie Mickle and Joan Oates in Virginia; Sara Armstrong in Mississippi; Anita Arnold and Vallene Cooks in Oklahoma; Carolyn Owens and Donna Rund in Indiana; Bess Fredlund in Montana; Susana Browne and Lei Ahsing in Hawaii; Shawn Powers in New Hampshire; and Teniqua Broughton, Laurie Little, Cheryl Mertz, Melissa Shaver, and Sheri Ulbrich in Arizona.

- Barbara Crowther for finding this work more important than sleeping in during her last year of college and for continuing her education so that she, too, can dramatize with students.

- All those teachers who attend my workshops and invite me into their classrooms because they still believe—even in today's test-driven educational climate—that their students deserve creative and compelling learning experiences.

- The students who continually show me that they really will invest in their learning if I do my job and make it active and meaningful for them.

- Corinne Mooney and Stacey Sharp, editors extraordinaire at the International Reading Association, for raising the bar for my writing and insisting that I deliver my best to the teachers who read this book.

- My colleagues for the continuing communication of your belief in me and my work—Sean Layne and Mauliola Cook, extreme e-mailers; Judy Thibault Klevins and Michael Bigley, steadfast supporters; Lenore Blank Kelner, tsunami superior; Marcia Daft, devoted divine one; and Stacey Coates, my amazing avid ace ally—for reading, revising, raving, and all the rest.

CHAPTER 1

Understanding Curriculum–Based Readers Theatre

What is Curriculum-Based Readers Theatre and why is it a valid instructional strategy?

Imagine a class of 10th-grade students standing in front of an audience in the classroom next door, the all-purpose room, or the school stage. These high school sophomores hold and perform a Readers Theatre script that they wrote based on the science topic "the water cycle." The students speak loudly and clearly. Some students speak solo lines; all students have the opportunity to speak lines in unison. They read fluently and with expression. All students perform gestures and sound effects to emphasize their words and add a visual element to the performance. They exhibit stage presence and concentration. Their performance of the script allows them, as well as their audience, to learn science content material in a fun and entertaining way.

THE WATER CYCLE

1: Coming soon to a theater near you...
All: [sound effect—scary movie theme music] The Water Cycle!
2: Watch as water goes from
All: liquid [sound effect] to gas. [sound effect]
3: The process known as
All: evaporation. [gesture]
4: Experience the rain, snow, and sleet that is
All: precipitation! [gesture]
2: [scream!]

1: And evaporation's reverse—
All: condensation! [gesture]
5: Resulting in...
6: [whispered] run-off
All: Not run-off! [gesture]
6: Run-off!
1: The surface water that runs into your
7: oceans,
8: ponds,
9: and rivers.
2: And don't forget run-off's arch enemy—
3: the treacherous

4–9: ground water!	**6:** a.k.a. "water."
All: [sound effect—gasp]	**1:** A Nourishing Life Film...
8: Starring Hydrogen and Oxygen,	**All:** "The Water Cycle!"
9: the dynamic duo known as	**7:** [sound effect—evil laugh]
All: H_2O! [sound effect]	

The audience watches and listens intently. Its members are delighted by the students' expressive reading, gestures, sound effects, and contemporary language. They are surprised to find themselves enjoying a presentation that includes facts and information. The audience has just experienced a Curriculum-Based Readers Theatre performance, and they applaud enthusiastically when the students finish.

What Is Curriculum-Based Readers Theatre?

Curriculum-Based Readers Theatre (Flynn, 2004/2005), or CBRT, is an instructional strategy that combines traditional Readers Theatre with creative writing to increase students' fluency, comprehension, and retention of information in any content area—whether it be English language arts, science, math, social studies, history, or any other content area that is part of a secondary education curriculum. With CBRT, students and teachers collaborate to take the contents of a textbook, work of literature, or almost any collection of facts and create scripts on these topics, allowing students to learn required material outlined in learning standards and assessment criteria in a way that is fun and engaging. In other words, CBRT is an arts-integrated instructional activity that allows teachers to dramatize content learning by infusing basic performance elements with classroom subject matter. However, neither teachers nor students need to be experienced with theater in order to successfully implement CBRT in the classroom.

The Traditional Readers Theatre Component of CBRT

Writing and performing scripts based on curriculum content expands the education uses of traditional Readers Theatre. Adams (2003) calls Readers Theatre "an activity by, of, and for readers, combining the act of reading with the techniques of theatre" (p. ix). The theatrical aspects of a traditional Readers Theatre performance occur through the readers or performers. They use their voices and facial expressions to communicate the content of the script that they hold in full view of the audience. They do not memorize the lines that they speak. Physical movement is minimal because Readers Theatre emphasizes spoken words, not staged scenes. There are no elaborate props, scenery, or costumes (Fredericks, 2001). Readers Theatre scripts allocate lines of dialogue to individual speakers, pairs, and small groups. They also contain lines spoken in unison or chorally by the entire group of performers.

Although advanced practitioners of Readers Theatre may incorporate theatrical elements such as stage movements, exits, and entrances, traditional Readers

Theatre staging is quite simple. Performers remain stationary in a straight line or semicircle, standing or seated on chairs or stools. Music stands or lecterns are sometimes used to hold the performers' scripts (Adams, 2003; Ratliff, 1999; Sloyer, 2003). Performers face the audience rather than looking at one another (Shepard, 1993; Walker, 1996). All performers remain in place as a group throughout the entire presentation; they do not make entrances and exits and move about the stage (Fredericks, 2001; Ratliff).

Stories and literature have customarily provided the content of Readers Theatre scripts (Adams, 2003; Black & Stave, 2007; Dixon, Davies, & Politano, 1996; Shepard, 1993; Sloyer, 2003). Many Readers Theatre print resources recommend or provide scripts based on quality literature (Black & Stave; Shepard), stories, novels, and poems; scenes from a play; song lyrics (Sloyer); narrative poems (Schneider, 2005); children's books (Wolf, 1993); short dramas and short stories (Tyler & Chard, 2000); letters, diaries, or other printed materials (Ratliff, 1999); or books with peppy dialogue, action, humor, lively narration, and enough parts for all speakers (Prescott, 2003).

Many authors endorse the use of Readers Theatre as a teaching and learning strategy for students of all ages (Adams, 2003; Dixon et al., 1996; Gustafson, 2002; Ratliff, 1999; Shepard, 1993; Sloyer, 2003; Walker, 1996). The reported benefits of classroom uses of literature-based Readers Theatre are many. Participation can encourage students to enjoy good literature and reading, engage with texts, adapt favorite stories, develop reading skills in the context of a cooperative and fun activity, interpret characters in scripts or stories, bring a text to life, present literary works in a dramatic form, introduce longer texts, seek books for silent reading, and apply reading comprehension skills including author's purpose, character traits, and mood and theme (see Badolato & Domanska, 2002; Kozub, 2000; Sebesta, n.d.; Shepard; Worthy & Prater, 2002). Teachers who find or create scripts of books or stories that pertain to their curricula report using them successfully with students—even students in middle school and high school (Larkin, 2001; Prescott, 2003; Schneider, 2005; Worthy & Prater).

Extending Readers Theatre Across Content Areas With CBRT

It is increasingly common to find books and articles that support moving Readers Theatre beyond the boundaries of stories and literature and using it to involve students in reading and speaking about curriculum content. Some resources provide ready-made scripts about topics such as scientific processes, the components of music, statistics, punctuation, multiplication, blood-borne pathogens, the Great Depression, the Vietnam War, or the first women's rights convention (Adams, 2003; Dixon et al., 1996; Fredericks, 2001; Gustafson, 2002; Harmon, Riney-Kehrberg, & Westbury, 1999). There is also ample encouragement in these resources for teachers to involve students in writing their own scripts about curriculum topics. Figure 1 provides just a sample of the variety of topics that can be explored through CBRT scripts. Each topic on this list comes from CBRT scripts developed in my work with students and teachers throughout the United States.

FIGURE 1. CBRT Script Topic Examples

Science
Electricity
Nutrition
Plants
Halley's Comet
Waves and Amplitude
Energy
Meteors
The Water Cycle

Literature
Number the Stars (Lowry)
Of Mice and Men (Steinbeck)
F. Scott Fitzgerald
The Great Migration (Lawrence)
Beowulf (Heaney)
To Kill a Mockingbird (Lee)
The Scarlet Letter (Hawthorne)
Shakespeare's Theater

Holes (Sachar)
Theme
Conflict
The View From Saturday (Konigsburg)
Characterization
Elements of a Story
Purposes for Reading
The Writing Process

Math
Bases and Exponents
Order of Operations
Range, Median, and Mode
Triangles
Polygons
Fractions

Grammar
Dangling Modifiers
Misplaced Modifiers

Parts of Speech
Onomatopoeia
Adjectives

Social Studies
The Bill of Rights
Explorers
Christopher Columbus
The Statue of Liberty
The Tower of London
Women's Suffrage
The Constitution
Renaissance Figures
The Constitutional Convention
Representation in Congress
Meso-Americans
The Civil War
Transcontinental Railroad

With CBRT, teachers and students create Readers Theatre scripts on topics that come directly from classroom curriculum content, not from published scripts or stories. *Reading Next: A Vision for Action and Research in Middle and High School Literacy* (Biancarosa & Snow, 2004) draws attention to the need for all subject matter teachers to use instructional approaches that will modify and enhance the curriculum content. CBRT scripts can focus on any curriculum area in which students are responsible for learning and retaining information.

The following sample script uses the CBRT format to present information about Readers Theatre and CBRT. (See Appendix A, page 82, for a reproducible version of this script.) You may want to give your students a broad introduction to CBRT by having them read this script aloud. It can also be used to inform colleagues, administrators, and parents about CBRT. This script is written for 10 solo speakers. The numbers that appear in the left-hand column indicate which solo speaker speaks which lines. Many Readers Theatre scripts use the format Reader 1, Reader 2, Reader 3, and so forth, but I find that eliminating the word "Reader" makes it easier for performers to locate their lines by visually scanning the text for the left-justified numeral.

CURRICULUM-BASED READERS THEATRE

By Rosalind M. Flynn

1: What is Readers Theatre?
2: Readers Theatre is a rehearsed

All: group presentation
3: of a script that is read aloud—

4:	NOT memorized.
5:	Performers hold their scripts throughout the performance.
6:	Lines are distributed among
7:	individuals,
8, 9:	pairs,
6–10:	small groups,
All:	and the whole group.
9:	Readers Theatre emphasizes spoken words,
10:	not staged scenes.
1:	So the performers don't move around the stage and enter and exit?
All:	Right!
1:	They just stand there and talk?
2:	Well, no. To make the performance more interesting, they add gestures that mean things like
3:	welcome [all wave],
4:	good idea [all give "thumbs up"],
5:	stop [all hold hand up with palm facing out],
6:	I don't know [all scratch heads].
7:	The performers also add sound effects to spice things up.
1:	Such as?
8:	Groans [all groan].
9:	Sighs [all sigh].
10:	Gasps [all gasp].
2:	Wind [all create wind sound].
3:	Falling rain [all slap thighs with palms].
4–7:	Music also adds to the entertainment value of Readers Theatre.

4:	For example, humming "London Bridge is Falling Down,"
All:	[begin and continue humming "London Bridge" under the words of the speakers]
4:	enlivens a script about Elizabethan England,
5:	the Globe Theater,
6:	and the dramatic works of William Shakespeare.
7:	So then—what's Curriculum-Based Readers Theatre?
8:	It's Readers Theatre that's based on curriculum content.
9:	It's scripts about facts and ideas that students are supposed to know.
10:	Curriculum-Based Readers Theatre involves students in
1:	researching,
2:	writing,
3:	revising,
4:	rehearsing,
5:	repeating,
6:	and performing a script meant to inform and entertain.
All:	Curriculum-Based Readers Theatre— [a rhythmic chant] A different, / creative, / dramatic teaching tool To work with information students need to learn in school.

How CBRT Scripts Are Developed

The development of a CBRT script often requires students to examine textbooks, information sheets, Web-based documents, or other content area texts. When they read content-rich materials, students must read for information; gather facts, details, and main points; and follow directions (Alliance for Excellent Education, 2006). Locating specific information, definitions, explanations, and examples to use in the scriptwriting gives students practice in content area reading and provides a purpose for the reading. The writing of the CBRT script offers students a creative way to represent their understanding of what they have read—to go beyond mere acquisition of content knowledge and make meaning of it for themselves and for others who will experience the performance of their script.

The following scripts are representative of the content, creativity, and contemporary flavor of CBRT scripts. The 11th graders who wrote the first script brainstormed ideas about the theme of friendship as found in John Steinbeck's *Of Mice and Men* (1993). (See Appendix A, page 83, for a reproducible version of this script.) Their scriptwriting assignment required them to do the following:

- Create a script that is at least two written pages long based on the theme of friendship in the novel.
- Identify/explain your theme.
- Include incidents from the book that demonstrate this theme.
- Include at least two quotes from the book.
- Describe Candy's friendship with his old dog.
- Describe George and Lennie's friendship.
- Be creative, interesting, humorous, and still factual in your writing.

THEMES IN *OF MICE AND MEN* BY JOHN STEINBECK

Developed with students at Yorktown High School, Arlington, Virginia, USA

1: *Of Mice and Men* is a novel about what's really valuable in life.

2: Yeah, like money!

All: Money! [gesture] Ch-ching!

3: No, like friends and family.

4: Money makes the world go round

5: and you know it!

6: Take an example from the book: How Crooks was poor...

7: He had no money.

All: Awwwwww. [gesture]

8: More importantly, Crooks had no one who cared about him.

9: It's like George said—"Guys like us got no fambly.... They ain't got nobody in the world that gives...

All: a hoot in hell about 'em!" [gesture]

10: Yeah, but even with a friend like Lennie, George is miserable without money.

11: But he's less miserable than others.... Take Candy, for example.

12: Candy had money saved, but the thing that made him happy was his friendship with...

All: his old dog. [sound effect]

1: So *Of Mice and Men* is more a story about friendship.

Evens: Candy and his dog.

Odds: George and Lennie.

13: George loves Lennie.

14: What? No he doesn't! He killed Lennie.

All: He killed him out of love. [gesture]

14: So? He still took another man's life!

13: He was doing Lennie a favor.

14: Why would you think that?

13: Because those other men would have killed him if George didn't do it himself.

15: Plus—he let Lennie die happily thinking of his dream.

All: "...we get that little place an' live on the fatta the lan'." [sound effect]

16: If the other guys killed him, Lennie would have died scared.

17: It was like putting a dog to sleep.

All: Yeah! [gesture]

18: But what about all the times George yelled at Lennie?

19:	And told him how much better his life would be without him?	**4:**	I know, but...
20:	He was just frustrated.	**All:**	"Maybe ever'body in the whole damn world is scared of each other."
1:	Besides, he had to put up with Lennie being clueless all the time.	**4:**	But...
2:	Lennie was simple-minded,	**All:**	"Funny how you and him string along together."
7:	but George is kind to Lennie...	**4:**	But you still wouldn't shoot your friend, would you?!
8:	because of his lack of intelligence.		
9:	And he never left him. He stuck by him.	**All:**	[gesture] Hmmmmmm....
All:	Like good friends do. [gesture]	**12:**	Lennie was just like Candy's poor dog.
4:	Well, I think George would have been much better off if he didn't have to deal with Lennie as a friend.	**13:**	He couldn't take care of himself.
		14:	He could no longer enjoy life.
10:	Well, you know what Crooks said—	**15:**	Just like...
All:	"A guy needs somebody to be near him."	**All:**	Lennie!
		16:	Lennie could not have enjoyed life, so George killed him.
4:	Yeah, but...	**17:**	He did it out of kindness.
All:	"He goes nuts if he ain't got nobody."	**18:**	He knew Lennie couldn't understand the consequences of his actions.
4:	Yeah, but...		
11:	And Slim said—	**4:**	Because in order to love your friends...
All:	"There's not many guys who travel around together."	**All:**	you've got to do what's best for them. [gesture]

The following math script was created by seventh graders and their teacher to reinforce the students' understanding of the rules for solving or simplifying mathematical expressions or equations. (See Appendix A, page 84, for a reproducible version of this script.)

THE ORDER OF OPERATIONS

Written by students at C.H.A.T. Academy, Selma, Alabama, USA

All:	What does 5 plus 2 times 3 equal?	**1:**	No, you don't have to do any of those. There is an easier way to do this. We will use a method called the order of operations.
1:	[gesture] I got it! It's 21.		
2:	[gesture and sound effect] Wrong answer. It's 11.		
All:	But both answers could be right. How can that be? [gesture]	**All:**	The order of operations? What's that? [gesture]
3:	Our teacher told us that there could only be one correct answer.	**2:**	The order of operations is a specific order for evaluating expressions so that we all get the same correct answer.
All:	How do we know which one is the right one?		
4:	Take a guess at it.	**All:**	How do we do the order of operations?
5:	Do "eenie meanie minie mo"?		
6:	Pray really hard.	**3:**	We do the order of operations in the following magnificent way.

4:	I am a grouping symbol.	**All:**	[chant]
All:	What's a grouping symbol?		Parentheses first!
4:	Grouping symbols are brackets, braces, and parentheses. You perform all operations within any of my symbols first.		Exponents next! Multiplication and division in the same step! [gesture] Addition and subtraction if you have the nerve—
5:	I am an exponent. You evaluate all my powers next.		From left to right, [gesture] First come, first serve [gesture]
6:	I am multiplication.		
7:	And I am division.	**10:**	One more time!
6, 7:	Perform any of our operations next.	**All:**	[chant]
All:	Going from left to right. [gesture]		Parentheses first!
8:	[prop] I am addition.		Exponents next!
9:	[prop] And I am subtraction.		Multiplication and division in the same
8, 9:	We're next in the order of operations.		step. [gesture]
All:	Going from left to right [gesture]		Addition and subtraction if you have
10:	To sum it up, there is a chant we can use. All together now.... And a 1...and a 2...and a 1, 2, 3....		the nerve— From left to right, [gesture] First come, first serve! [gesture]

What Makes CBRT
a Valid Instructional Strategy?

CBRT is a learning activity that directly addresses standards of learning and increases reading fluency—and therefore comprehension—as students participate in an authentic purpose for reading and writing across the content areas. The repetition of content information required by CBRT rehearsals enhances students' retention of facts and information. CBRT is an arts-integrated instructional activity with the potential to increase students' academic achievement while motivating and engaging them in a positive learning experience.

Reading Fluency and Comprehension

Reading educators have long endorsed the classroom use of traditional Readers Theatre to strengthen reading fluency—the ability to read a text accurately and quickly (Fountas & Pinnell, 2001; Martinez, Roser, & Strecker, 1998; Rasinski, 2000; Scraper, 2005). Fluent readers read aloud smoothly and with expression. They recognize words and understand them at the same time. Fluency is an important skill in reading any kind of text—literary or informational content material—because of the close relationship between fluency and comprehension. Fluent readers tend to comprehend what they read and become higher achieving students (Fountas & Pinnell; Rasinski, 2000, 2006). The repeated oral reading required in rehearsals and performances of CBRT and Readers Theatre increases students' public speaking skills, oral expression, and reading fluency.

Most important, however, is that fluent readers understand what they read as they read it. Their reading proficiency directly contributes to successful comprehension of the texts they read in all curriculum areas. Fluency, therefore, is central to and essential for reading comprehension (Pikulski, 2006). Because of this close relationship between fluency and comprehension, fluent readers tend to be higher achieving students (Fountas & Pinnell, 2001; Rasinski, 2000, 2006).

Fluency is most apparent and observable when students read orally. Fluent readers speak with appropriate speed, expression, phrasing, intonation, and prosody (stress and rhythm) while reading (Allington, 2006; Rasinski, 2006). Pikulski (2006) calls oral reading "vitally important because it is an observable reflection of decoding and fluency" (p. 71). Expressive reading, therefore, is not important just for its own sake; it is important because it contributes to gains in reading achievement (Rasinski).

Reading the same passage several times orally is an effective strategy for developing reading fluency because repeated reading provides the practice needed for reading to become automatic (Samuels, 1979/1997). *Automaticity* refers to the ability "to perform two different skills at the same time as the result of extended practice" (Samuels, 2006, p. 39). When the two different skills of decoding words and comprehending words occur simultaneously, at least one of them is automatic (Samuels, 2006). When students decode words automatically, they are more likely to understand what they read. When they reread a passage several times, as they will reread their lines with CBRT, they make fewer errors and they read more quickly (Samuels, 2006). In reviews of research related to repeated readings, Dowhower (in Rasinski, 2006) reports that students who engaged in repeated readings of the same material showed improvements in reading rate and word-recognition accuracy, and comprehension of both literal and higher level information. Repeated readings were also an effective study strategy for these same students.

CBRT provides a purpose for reading the same text orally over and over again because the text is a script, and a script requires rehearsal. It is not unusual for students to rehearse the same script 15 to 20 times to prepare for performance. Rasinski (2000) calls Readers Theatre a "natural and authentic way to promote repeated readings" (p. 148). Samuels (2006) agrees and includes Readers Theatre in his collection of oral reading methods for developing fluency, calling it a "real-life" reason to do repeated readings (p. 30). Tyler and Chard (2000) find Readers Theatre especially suitable to the needs and abilities of struggling readers because it offers an acceptable, legitimate reason to reread the same text several times.

Dowhower (in Rasinski, 2006) reports that repeated reading improves fluency not only in the practiced text but also in unpracticed passages. Georges (2005b) agrees, reporting specific support for the use of CBRT to improve and extend students' oral reading fluency. Sixth-grade students participating in his study rehearsed and performed three CBRT scripts. Rehearsals focused on pronunciation, definitions, inflection, rate of speech, posture, cue pick-up, teamwork, sound effects, and gestures. One week after the CBRT intervention, the students were tested and showed significant improvement in oral reading of a new text.

Readers Theatre is an instructional strategy that motivates the repeated, modeled, and coached oral reading that promotes comprehension (Stahl & Kuhn, 2002). The ensemble reading and speaking experience gives less skilled or struggling readers fluency support from more capable readers. When others read solo lines aloud, all students benefit by concurrently looking at the text and hearing fluent reading (Martinez et al., 1998; Rasinski, 2001). When readers speak lines with others, they see, vocalize, and hear words simultaneously. As part of this group speaking experience, they practice correct pronunciation, intonation, phrasing, and expression. CBRT, therefore, broadens these Readers Theatre benefits for students by providing oral practice that enhances students' reading fluency while also merging writing, reading, curricular topics, and theatrical skills.

The state of Florida requires teachers to complete fluency checks for struggling readers. In a study of my CBRT work by the Kennedy Center Partners in Education Professional Development Project (2006), some participating teachers chose to study whether their students' fluency would increase as a result of participating in CBRT. They reported that the reading fluency of 100% of their students improved by an average increase of 17 words per minute.

Differentiating Instruction

CBRT also offers a variety of approaches to differentiated instruction. A whole class can work together in the teacher-led writing, rehearsing, and performing of a script. Once they are familiar with CBRT, students who are more motivated or capable can work individually or in small groups to write a CBRT script. By providing such

CBRT IN ACTION

Because I am a visiting artist, I am unfamiliar with the students' academic ability levels when I begin my work with them in a residency session. Therefore, I distribute the solo parts in a sample CBRT script with no preconceived notion of which students are the good readers. I explain that a solo part means that you will read alone and then I ask for volunteers and I hand out the scripts. Again and again, I have experienced scenes similar to the following one:

The first solo speaker struggles through the delivery of the opening line with choppy reading, incorrect pronunciations, and little to no oral expression. I am puzzled as to why this student chose to speak a solo part. I help him or her get through this line and the other lines in the first read-through of the script. The second read-through shows improvement. In the third read-through, this same student (and the other speakers, too) reads the solo lines clearly, smoothly, and with effective expression.

After class the teacher expresses amazement at how well her students did with the CBRT script. "Even some of my resource kids were participating and volunteering to read out loud and they never do that."

students with a scriptwriting assignment, teachers can challenge them to focus on the same curriculum material that other students may need to move through more slowly or with additional teacher guidance. The script writers concentrate on the same information, but in a different way. They deepen their understanding of the topic by considering how to present its facts in script form and by writing, reading, and revising their script. Their scriptwriting is an example of what Tomlinson (2001) endorses as providing a different approach to "*what* students learn, *how* they learn it, and how they *demonstrate what they've learned*" (pp. 4–5). The CBRT script that an individual or small group creates may then be shared with the whole class to rehearse and perform. This use of CBRT confirms Tomlinson's pattern of instruction in a differentiated classroom as "a blend of whole-class, group, and individual instruction" (p. 5).

Repetition Enhances Retention

Rehearsals of a CBRT script result in students repeatedly reading and hearing content information. The term "rehearsal" is a learning strategy as well as a theatrical practice. Basic rehearsal learning strategies refer to the learner's active reciting, repeating, or naming of presented items during learning (Weinstein & Mayer, 1986).

Why can most actors recite entire speeches they made in plays years ago although they may not be able to recall the ingredients of a recipe they made just last week? It has to do with the repetition of material that is involved in rehearsal. Reading the script silently, then reciting it orally, and repeating and reviewing that information through rehearsals lead to the retention of that material. This experience can be summed up with the following formula: Reading + Recitation + Repetition + Review = Retention. Actors remember what they read and rehearse in preparation for performance. A test is also a performance. Dramatizing curriculum content with CBRT is one way to rehearse for improved test results. Participation in CBRT encourages the retention of facts and concepts due to the repetition involved first in writing and later in reading, rehearsing, and performing the scripted information.

Many standards of learning expect students to retain information that requires what Jensen (1998) calls semantic memory. It's the type of memory that involves words—names, facts, figures, and textbook information; it is the weakest of human beings' retrieval systems. Rehearsal, review, and reactivation strengthen semantic memory. It is difficult to get students to read or listen to a reading of the same content material 10 to 15 times. Script the information as CBRT and rehearsals become an accepted part of the process. The orally repeated content eventually becomes reflexive or automatic. Ideally, rehearsal and repetition (like practicing the multiplication tables out loud) cause the content to enter the long-term memory, retained for performance and assessment.

In one study, Georges (2005a) found that the use of CBRT science scripts by sixth graders resulted in students retaining the science content of the scripts equally as well as peers who received traditional science instruction. The students who learned the content through traditional science instruction, however, spent a total of 36 instructional hours over two months, compared with the group that learned the same material via the CBRT scripts in only 28 instructional hours. This difference of 8 hours was significantly less time than that required by traditional science instruction. From the perspective of the teacher involved in the study, science instruction (as measured by responses on a written test) through CBRT proved a significantly more efficient method of instruction.

Trainin and Andrzejczak (2006) conducted three studies in which the Readers Theatre component was scripts based on classroom curriculum. They found that the use of scripting techniques by students and teachers led to longer reading periods and more contact with the curriculum texts, and ultimately to increased student performance in both fluency and comprehension. In addition, some teachers in the Kennedy Center Partners in Education Professional Development Project (2006) studied their students' retention of content vocabulary after participation in CBRT. They reported that 80% of their students showed a 39% increase in retention of vocabulary terminology.

CBRT is also one example of the arts functioning as a way of committing concepts and content to memory:

> This experience brings subjects alive for learners by incorporating a wide array of compelling visual, aural, tactile, and kinesthetic activities into the generation of new knowledge, thereby providing enough vivid sense memories to make new learning memorable (literally able to be remembered). These indelible sensory images mark and organize information and concepts in a way that allows learners to access and apply new knowledge. (Burnaford, Aprill, & Weiss, 2001, pp. 11–12)

In other words, learners must actively engage with concepts and content.

Arts Integration

It is the artistic aspect of the CBRT process that distinguishes this type of repeated reading from a class read-aloud or the one-time reading of a traditional Readers Theatre script. The writing and reading that students do in CBRT involve them in

CBRT IN ACTION

I had worked with a sixth-grade social studies class in Sarasota, Florida, to develop a CBRT script on the topic of culture. Two months later, I made a return visit to the same class and worked with the students and their teacher on a new script. At the end of the class period, I said to the students, "By the way, I know it's been a while, but does anyone here remember what a culture is?" Without skipping a beat and in unison, they all replied, "Culture—the way of life of people, including their beliefs, customs, and practices—yeah!"

the work that playwrights, directors, actors, and critics do. Emphasizing the theatrical skills and products of CBRT turns this classroom learning process into an arts-integration experience.

Integration happens when two separate elements are combined into one cohesive whole. In arts-integrated learning, the art form becomes an interdisciplinary partner with another subject or subjects. Arts integration is designed to promote transfer of learning between an art form and other subjects (Rabkin, 2004). The curriculum content area provides the topic while the art form provides the "ways and means." Students engage in a rich array of skills and learning strategies so that the understandings of each content area—both the art form and the curriculum subject—are enriched and illuminated by the presence of the other (Burnaford et al., 2001). The results are mutually beneficial: The arts enhance learning in other subjects while their infiltration into other subjects improves learning in the arts (Fowler, 1996).

Each art form is rooted in specific content. In other words, the arts are all about *something.* Consider the art form of theater. Think, for example, of the vast amount of research about the events surrounding the U.S. Declaration of Independence required to create the script, songs, set, and costumes for the Broadway musical *1776.* That's arts integration on a huge professional scale—specific historical content explored via musical and theatrical means. In CBRT, curriculum topics provide the subject matter for the scripts; the art form of theater provides the processes, products, and motivation for the work involving the information.

Grumet (2004) sums up the value of arts integration most eloquently. She writes that "programs integrating the arts with the rest of the academic curriculum show that we learn what thrills us with risk, what warms us with applause, what beckons us to learn just over the edge of the familiar, what comforts us with harmony and resolution" (p. 61). CBRT has the potential to involve students and teachers in a meaningful, but accessible, arts-integration experience.

Furthermore, CBRT can allow teachers and students to address difficult, sensitive, or even controversial issues at a comfort level that may not be possible with traditional instruction. The CBRT script provides a dramatic context and everyone understands that the lines of dialogue exist to communicate perspectives and viewpoints particular to the issue being studied, not to the individuals presenting the performance. Students may deliver lines that express sentiments that they do not condone. For example, the sample scripts on segregation and women's suffrage provided on pages 79 and 81 in Appendix A allow students to address sensitive topics from several outdated viewpoints and provide a safe dramatic approach to the topics without offending anyone.

Student Engagement and Motivation

Using curriculum content as the focus of a classroom arts activity makes sense, both practically and in terms of students' positive participation. Grumet (2004) endorses arts integration as one answer for educators trying to transform the passivity that characterizes students in many classrooms: "In integration programs, students reveal enthusiasms and hidden capacities, and express ideas, feelings, and new dimensions of their intelligence" (p. 51). The arts summon students' personal involvement and motivate them to want to learn and be excited by their learning (Fowler, 1996). Arts integration is a viable strategy for engaging students more fully with the traditional academic curriculum (Weissman, 2004) and providing a purpose for the meaningful learning that occurs best when students are actively engaged (Burnaford et al., 2001).

The need for students' engagement in their learning found in the arts-integration literature echoes the same issue emphasized in *Reading Next: A Vision for Action and Research in Middle and High School Literacy* (Biancarosa & Snow, 2004). "The proportion of students who are not engaged or motivated by their school experiences grows at every grade level and reaches epidemic proportions in high school" (p. 9). The authors emphasize the need for all subject matter teachers to build motivation to read and learn by choosing from a variety of instructional approaches to enhance the curriculum content. CBRT is one available choice.

In various stages of the CBRT writing, reading, and rehearsing process, actively engaged students exhibit what Rabkin and Redmond (2004) call "The Look" (p. 127). Students sit on the edge of their seats, eyes focused forward. They watch and listen to one another and the teacher, strain to contribute ideas, smile, laugh, and squint as if they are squeezing new thoughts out of their heads. They show physical evidence of their deep engagement in the lesson that is taking place.

Professional actors prepare and rehearse for hours and hours because they love the process, the people, and the performance. Many students do, too. Schneider (2005), who teaches seventh and eighth graders, finds that more than ever, students enjoy performing and bringing their reading alive in class. "Readers Theatre certainly makes the classroom lively, and hearing good language is essential for young readers" (p. 55).

Ownership of Script Material. Part of the deep engagement in CBRT experiences can be attributed to the students' experience of ownership of the script they create, rehearse, and perform. The script is their understanding and communication of the topic being studied. The words, phrases, voices, gestures, humor, and sound effects are their creations. Exploring curriculum content through the art form of theater draws students into the subject matter and gives them ownership of it (Fowler, 1996). This aspect of CBRT is also a way to address one of the 15 elements of effective adolescent literacy programs proposed by *Reading Next: A Vision for Action and Research in Middle and High School Literacy* (Biancarosa & Snow, 2004). The report recommends text-based collaborative learning, a strategy in which students interact with one another around a text. This approach to a text or a topic gives students concrete problems to discuss or solve and involves them in making meaning through a group process.

Stevenson and Deasy (2005) confirm the power of student-centered teaching and learning through the arts. The students they discuss in their book *Third Space: When Learning Matters* participated in arts learning experiences that engaged them in different and more powerful ways than other school programs in their

CBRT IN ACTION

It was my first CBRT residency session with an eighth-grade class in rural Maryland. In the back of the classroom sat a boy whose slouching posture, disdainful facial expression, and cynical comments clearly communicated that he was much too "cool" for this kind of activity. I forged on, developing a script with his classmates, hoping his resistance would not influence the other students. This boy, however, began to perk up when he realized that I was actually going to allow the students to have lots of input to this script about purposes for reading. He became amused and quite attentive when some of the lines in the script incorporated slang particular to that school, especially a phrase that he contributed.

On my second day of work with this class, the change in this boy's attitude shocked even me. The students and I had photocopies of the first draft of our script. As we read through it to make changes and additions, this boy began participating earnestly. He contributed ideas for lines, gestures, and sound effects, carefully recording the changes on his own script. He asked me to slow down and repeat words so that he could copy them down correctly. By the end of that class, as the bell rang, this boy had left his seat to come to the front of the class to compare his script with mine to be sure that his was accurate. I tried not to look as amazed as I felt as I watched him engaged in the work in ways that I never would have imagined at the start of the residency.

economically disadvantaged communities. Learning with and through the arts became something that mattered to these students who felt involved, empowered, and effective. Georges (2005b) found the same positive sentiments expressed by students who participated in CBRT. Interviewed students expressed confidence in their ability to produce a CBRT script themselves and identified numerous other subjects that could be scripted as CBRT. One sixth grader announced that CBRT made her want to come to school more often. "If I knew we were doing Readers Theatre the next day, I didn't miss it" (p. 1).

Authentic Audience. Another motivating factor for students engaged in arts activities like CBRT is the potential audience for their creation. Before beginning a CBRT script, students must ask, "Who will be reading and listening to this writing?" CBRT scriptwriting focuses students' attention on this element of writing because what they write will be read aloud—performed—for an actual audience. "Is our audience children? Peers? Middle school students? High school students? Adults? What appeals to our particular audience? How can we deliver factual information in entertaining ways for this audience?" According to Stevenson and Deasy (2005), "The prospect of exhibiting or performing their art work endows the arts learning experience with a purpose that focuses energies and heightens the importance of its challenges, adding another dimension to the power of the arts to matter to students" (p. 28). Typically, students' work has an audience of one: the teacher. The audience for a CBRT script and performance can be far greater. Whether the performance is for the class next door or an auditorium full of family and friends, audiences motivate students. Raising the stakes for student work by providing an audience has a powerful effect (Weissman, 2004).

With the goal of performing for an audience, students are motivated to repeat and review even the least compelling curriculum content. Bidwell (in McMaster, 1998) agrees, noting that reading something over and over may sound good to the researchers, but students need a reason to want to reread. Students understand the need to rehearse a script many times to be prepared to perform in front of a real audience.

SCRIPT SECTION: PURPOSES FOR READING

1: Ugh! Here's a book my teacher's forcing me to read!

2: I wish we could vote on a book we want to read.

3: Like Emmitt Smith's biography! [gesture]

4: Slash and gash thrillers! [sound effect] [gesture]

5: Edgar Allan Poe poetry!

6: *One Fish, Two Fish, Red Fish, Blue Fish!*

All: [sound effect]

7: So why can't we just choose our own books?

8: Or not read at all? [sound effect]

9: We have to read for literary experience.

All: Why? [gesture]

10: Our teachers make us.

11: The Board of Education says so.

12: It will expand our vocabulary.

13: We can move to a higher level of thinking.

14: Yeah, yeah, yeah...my teacher is always telling us the purposes for reading.

All: [sound effect]

15: Right—in Language Arts, we read Rip Van Winkle for

All: literary experience. [gesture]

16: Whad'ja think?

1: It was so-so.

2: I didn't like it! The words were too big and boring!

10: I thought the pictures were cool.

3: OK, but sometimes if you use strategies, it helps you with your reading.

Increased Student Achievement. Reports and studies of arts-integration programs also provide evidence that when arts experiences are connected to academic instruction, student achievement is sustained and increased, not diminished, by this enriched curriculum (Grumet, 2004; Rabkin, 2004; Weissman, 2004). In a report published by the Arts Education Partnership, *Champions of Change: The Impact of the Arts on Learning* (Fiske, 2000), researchers describe benefits that directly support use of the art form of theater. Sustained student involvement in theater arts was associated with gains in reading proficiency, self-concept and motivation, and higher levels of empathy and tolerance for others (Catterall, Chapleau, & Iwanaga, 2000). Project Zero, an educational research group at the Graduate School of Education at Harvard University, examined 80 studies on classroom drama (enacting texts) and a variety of verbal areas. The report on Project Zero's findings—REAP (Reviewing Education and the Arts Project)—concludes that participation in drama helps to build verbal skills that also transfer to new materials (Podlozny, 2001).

Addressing Standards of Learning

CBRT invites the integration of a variety of local, state, or national standards (in any subject area) into an arts learning activity. On the broadest level, the writing aspect of CBRT addresses writing content standards such as standard 5 of the *Standards for the English Language Arts* (International Reading Association [IRA] & National Council of Teachers of English [NCTE], 1996):

> 5. Students employ a wide range of strategies as they write and use different writing process elements appropriately to communicate with different audiences for a variety of purposes.

Script topics can directly correspond with curriculum standards for any course of study. With their Bill of Rights Readers Theatre script (see Appendix A, page 74), for example, a sixth-grade class addressed part of the third National History Standard. Standard 3B requires that "the student understands the guarantees of the Bill of Rights and its continuing significance" (National Center for History in the Schools, 1996).

CBRT IN ACTION

I conducted a CBRT residency in the class of a social studies teacher responsible for helping her students meet the Virginia Standard of Learning requiring students to identify the basic principles of the new government established by the Constitution of the United States and the Bill of Rights. She explained that her students would need to pass a state test including this information and she really wanted them to do well. Together, she and her students and I developed a script that explained the first 10 Amendments to the Constitution—the Bill of Rights.

During the five hour-long classes I met with them, we wrote, read, revised, rehearsed, and performed the script for three other social studies classes. The residency ended, and a couple of months later I was back at this same school to present a teacher workshop. I was setting up when I heard a loud gasp and felt my arm being squeezed in excitement by the teacher from my residency. She had just received her students' test scores. "They passed!" she exclaimed. "They know the Bill of Rights! They passed the test!"

The CBRT script portion on page 1 of this chapter addresses one aspect of Earth and Space Science Content Standard D of the National Science Education Standards:

> As a result of their activities in grades 9–12, all students should develop an understanding of geochemical cycles. In grades 9–12, students review the water cycle as a carrier of material and deepen their understanding of this key cycle to see that it is also an important agent for energy transfer. (National Research Council, 1996)

Because CBRT places audience at the forefront of students' writing considerations and therefore directly addresses one of the standards for English language arts:

> 4. Students adjust their use of spoken, written, and visual language (e.g., conventions, style, vocabulary) to communicate effectively with a variety of audiences and for different purposes. (IRA & NCTE, 1996)

The United States No Child Left Behind Act of 2001 includes the arts in its definition of core academic subjects (Arts Education Partnership, 2005). CBRT, therefore, by merging writing and content learning with the art form of theater, also addresses aspects of the National Standards for Arts Education Theater Content Standard 4:

> Grades 5–8
>
> Directing by organizing rehearsals for improvised and scripted scenes:
>
> Students lead small groups in planning visual and aural elements and in rehearsing improvised and scripted scenes, demonstrating social, group, and consensus skills.
>
> Grades 9–12
>
> Directing by interpreting dramatic texts and organizing and conducting rehearsals for informal or formal productions:
>
> Students justify selections of text, interpretation, and visual and aural artistic choices. (Consortium of National Arts Education Associations, 1994).

The next chapter details how you can introduce CBRT and begin to create scripts with your students.

CHAPTER 2

Beginning Curriculum-Based Readers Theatre

How do you introduce Curriculum-Based Readers Theatre to students?

This chapter presents a sequence of activities that you, the teacher, lead students through only once. This introduction to the practice of using gestures and sound effects in Readers Theatre and the experience of reading through a sample Curriculum-Based Readers Theatre script set the stage for all future CBRT work.

The CBRT Instructional Schedule in Figure 2 provides an overview of the sequence and pacing of all of the components of CBRT over five sessions. Although the elements of the chart will be clearer as you continue reading this book, it is included here to give you a sense of the instructional time involved. The schedule outlines a five-session process of introducing CBRT and its conventions; brainstorming information for a model CBRT script; beginning, continuing, revising, and completing the model CBRT script; and rehearsing the script in preparation for performance.

Begin the introduction to CBRT by explaining to students that they will be working with you to learn about Readers Theatre in order to write an original Readers Theatre script based on a content area topic. Discuss any background knowledge or previous experience of Readers Theatre with the group, but keep your explanation of Readers Theatre simple. Emphasize, primarily, that it's a kind of theatrical presentation in which the performers always hold and read from their scripts. What separates Readers Theatre from boring, monotonous reading aloud from a paper, however, is the expressive use of voices and the incorporation of gestures and sound effects.

Conventions: In theatrical performance, practices accepted as part of the dramatic experience. In musical theater, for example, the audience accepts the convention that all the characters break into a song and dance and they all know the words and the steps, which they perform together perfectly.

Practicing Readers Theatre Conventions

Beginning your introduction to CBRT with the theatrical elements, or **conventions**, of CBRT is a practical starting point and also a great

FIGURE 2. CBRT Instructional Schedule

Day 1	Day 2	Day 3	Day 4	Day 5
Introduce CBRT and its conventions:* • Gestures • Sound effects • Gestures and sound effects together Share a sample CBRT script:* • "Stumble-through" • Second read-through • Third read-through • Examine the sample script for entertaining and informational elements. *The above introductory steps are only needed for the students' first exposure to CBRT.* Introduce topic for model CBRT script: • Brainstorm and list information to include in the original script that you and students will create together.	Continue brainstorming and listing information for the model CBRT script. Begin the model CBRT script: • Consider possible contexts and characters. • Write the opening lines. • Record the lines. • Read through and add to the script.	Continue the model CBRT script: • Record more lines. • Read through, add to, and complete the first draft of the script. If appropriate, have students work on writing script sections in small groups. Type up the first draft of the model CBRT script. *The collaborative model CBRT script may be a one-time activity used to teach students the CBRT writing process.*	Photocopy and distribute the first draft of the model CBRT script. Assign lines for a read-through and have students highlight their lines. With students, read through and revise the first draft of the model CBRT script. Ascertain how many students wish to speak solo lines in the final draft of the model CBRT script. Type up revised final draft of the model CBRT script.	Photocopy and distribute the final draft of the model CBRT script. Assign permanent lines and have students highlight their lines. Begin rehearsing the spoken words, sound effects, and gestures. Assign stage positions and continue rehearsing. Coach for projection, articulation, energy, and expression. Review entering and exiting the performance space. Rehearse until you are satisfied that the students are ready to perform.

Note. Each day represents a 50- to 60-minute class period.

opportunity to build students' interest and enthusiasm for the project. By having students demonstrate these conventions themselves, they will not only be "learning by doing" (as discussed in the Preface on page ix), but also they will become easily engaged in the CBRT process. In CBRT, the conventions employed require no theatrical background or experience. They are familiar everyday enhancements to communication—gestures and sound effects.

Gestures

Begin with the meaning of the word *gesture*. If students are not familiar with the term, assure them that they communicate with and respond to gestures every day. Demonstrate in this way: Make eye contact with one student and gesture that he or she should (1) come stand beside you, (2) turn around in a circle, (3) bow, and (4) return to his or her seat. Then gesture that the other students should applaud.

Once students understand that gestures are a silent means of communicating with arms, fingers, faces, and body, invite all students simultaneously to practice communicating without words. Use Figure 3 as a guide. Tell students that you will read the words or phrases aloud and together they will communicate what you read through gestures alone—no sounds allowed.

During this activity, praise and point out the variety of gestures students perform to communicate the same message. "Let me think," for example, can be gestured by scratching the head or by stroking the chin with the thumb and forefinger.

Praise students' inevitable uses of the appropriate facial expressions accompanying their gestures. The "I've got an idea" gesture is performed with an enthusiastic facial expression, not a bored or sleepy one. Emphasize how gestures allow people to communicate without making a sound. When gestures are used to emphasize the words in a CBRT performance, the result is a more dramatic and visually compelling presentation.

FIGURE 3. Gestures Practice Sheet

Ask students to use gestures—no noise or words—to communicate the following ideas:

• Come here.	• OK!	• Salute
• Good idea.	• Stop.	• What do you mean?
• What time is it?	• Cut it out.	• I'm hungry.
• I don't know.	• I hope so!	• I'm waiting.
• How surprising!	• Be quiet.	• Pay attention.
• Let me think.	• Maybe. So-so.	• Hurry up.
• No.	• Look over there.	• That hurts.
• That's crazy!	• I'm tired.	• Knock on the door.
• Please!	• Forget about it.	• Scolding "Unh, unh, unh!"
• I've got an idea!	• Bye.	• Call me on the phone.
• Talk to the hand.	• My lips are sealed.	• Make a toast.
• Yes!	• I've got a headache.	

Sound Effects

Following the gestures activity, explain that a Readers Theatre performance also becomes more interesting with the incorporation of sound effects. This term rarely has to be defined for students, so, immediately after practicing gestures, involve them in producing sound effects as a group. See Figure 4 for a list of sound effect prompts. If necessary, create and demonstrate a gesture that you (the teacher) will perform to indicate that the sound effect production should stop (such as the arm and hand movements performed by an orchestra leader).

Gestures and Sound Effects Together

Next, invite students to perform gestures and sound effects together. Remind students of the gesture you will perform when the group is to stop all noise and movement, and then cue them with the gesture and sound effect prompts provided in Figure 5.

You may continue by adding your own or students' ideas for gestures and sound effects. The ultimate goal of these introductory activities is for students to understand that the performance of their Readers Theatre scripts will be enhanced—made more theatrical—by incorporating gestures and sound effects.

FIGURE 4. Sound Effects Practice Sheet

Ask all students in unison to create the following sound effects:

- groans
- sighs
- gasps
- wind
- water
- a haunted house
- a freezing temperature
- a door creaking open
- soldiers marching
- a door slamming shut
- horses galloping
- a clock ticking
- an alarm clock sounding

- a truck backing up
- church bells
- a jolly laugh
- an evil laugh
- "glugging" a drink
- steam escaping
- a siren
- sounds people make when they feel
  - amazed
  - skeptical
  - surprised
  - touched or heart-warmed

- pleased
- shocked
- admiration
- puzzled
- frustrated
- joyful (or ecstatic)
- sleepy (or lethargic)
- annoyed (or perturbed)
- fearful (or filled with trepidation)
- angry (or vexed)
- triumphant (or smug)
- puzzled (or bewildered)

FIGURE 5. Gestures and Sound Effects Practice Sheet

Ask all students in unison to create the gestures and sound effects for the following items:

- a wrong answer
- a right answer
- a good taste
- a bad smell

- an amazing sight
- a sorrowful farewell
- a boring program
- a scolding parent

- enthusiastic fans
- revving an engine
- slurping soup
- shivering cold

Sharing a Sample CBRT Script

Reading a sample script is what really clarifies CBRT for students. Photocopy one script for each student. For younger students, you may want to identify each speaker's lines by highlighting them with a marker before you distribute the scripts. Older students can highlight their own lines. Distribute the scripts, assign the solo parts to volunteer readers, and give everyone a few minutes to review their lines and inquire about pronunciations or other concerns. Explain that the numbers in the left-hand column indicate which speaker speaks which line. Lines assigned to "All" involve the whole class speaking in unison. Words or phrases in brackets are **stage directions**.

> **Stage Directions:** Instructions to the performers that are not meant to be spoken aloud.

The following script serves well as a sample introductory script for middle school students. The script has solo parts and multiple lines for all students. (See Appendix A, page 85, for a reproducible version of this script.)

THE MIDDLE COLONIES

Developed with students at Wood Middle School, Rockville, Maryland, USA

1:	Ladies and Gentlemen...[sound effect]
2:	Introducing [sound effect]
1–5:	Not the New England
6–10:	Not the Southern
All:	But...the Middle Colonies
3:	Based on a chapter in YOUR Social Studies book
All:	*The United States* [gesture]
1–5:	*Its History*
6–10:	*and Neighbors*
4:	Written by
All:	Us [gesture]
5:	Starring
All:	New York, New Jersey, Delaware, and Pennsylvania! [gesture]
6:	also known as
6–10:	"The Breadbasket Colonies"
7:	Why?
Girls:	[Rap] We're the breadbasket girls and we're here to say, "Our colonies bake bread on every day. Our fields yield crops of beautiful wheat and other things most excellent to eat!"
8:	What do you call a person who owned and ruled a Middle Colony?
9:	A delegate?

All:	No! A proprietor.
9:	Then what's a delegate?
All:	Delegates were people elected by colonists to represent them in colonial assemblies.
6, 7:	Have you ever heard of Sarah Knight?
10:	Isn't she the lady on *Good Morning America*?
All:	[sound effect] [gesture]
6:	No! She made a journey by horseback from Boston to New York City in 1704.
7:	She wrote about how difficult it was to travel the rocky roads and cross the rivers.
1:	When Sarah Knight visited New York, the Dutch influence was still strong.
2:	What's *influence*?
All:	*Influence* means the power of people or things to act on others.
2:	Oh. Could you give me an example of Dutch influence?
3:	Did you ever hear of a Dutch door?
2:	Nope.
4:	Well, it's a door with two parts. The top part could be open while the bottom part stays closed.

2:	Cool.	8:	Not. Pigs were used for cleaning up the garbage people threw in their gutters in the cities.
8:	Hey, I bet you don't know what pigs were used for in colonial cities!		
10:	Duh. They were used for pets.	All:	Yuck! [gesture]

For both middle school and high school students, the "Halley's Comet" script works well as an introductory script. Like "The Middle Colonies" script, it has solo parts and multiple lines for students. (See Appendix A, page 86, for a reproducible version of this script.)

HALLEY'S COMET

Developed with students at John F. Kennedy High School, Richmond, Virginia, USA

1:	Attention everyone! The planets and their satellites are the most noticeable members of the sun's family.	7:	How long has Halley's comet been around?
All:	Thanks for the news flash.	2:	Since our grandparents were kids. [sound effect]
1:	Let me finish. But there are many other objects in the solar system.	8:	Longer. Since the dinosaurs.
All:	Like what? [gesture]	9:	When was the last time anyone saw it?
1:	Have you ever heard of Halley's comet?	10:	In 1986. It's only seen from Earth every 76 years. [sound effect] [gesture]
2:	I have.	2:	So we won't be able to see it again until...
3:	What is it?		
2:	Halley's comet is just a big dusty snowball.	All:	2062.
4:	Big deal.	6:	Man, our grandchildren will be digging our graves then!
1:	Wait—what's in this big dusty snowball?	All:	[gesture] Maybe. Maybe not.
5:	I know that answer. A comet has dust and rock particles mixed with frozen water.	3:	Hey, if we're still here the next time Halley's comet rolls around, I'll bring the chips.
6:	And don't forget the methane and ammonia.	4:	And I'll bring the dip.
All:	Methane and ammonia. [sound effect] [gesture]	5:	And we'll watch that dusty snowball from our comfortable wheelchairs!
		All:	2062—be there! [gesture] [sound effect]

Emphasizing Cues

During the reading or performing of any script, actors need to be aware of **cues**. When they prepare for a role, actors study not only the lines they will speak and the actions they will execute, but also when they will speak and move. Before beginning the read-throughs, alert students to be aware of their cues as well as their lines.

Cue: On stage, an actor's "cue" refers to any words, sounds, or movements that signal the start of a new line, sound, o movement.

Conducting Read-Throughs of the Sample CBRT Script

Begin your first **read-through**. Pause wherever you see *[gesture]* or *[sound effect]* and help the students decide what movement or sound to perform. You will need to remind them that because they will be holding their Readers Theatre scripts in one hand (usually the left, but this is a matter of teacher or student preference), their gestures will generally be performed primarily with the other hand and arm.

It's best to solicit and use students' ideas for vocal expression, gestures, and sound effects, but do establish yourself as director. Maintain your right to veto any suggestions you find inappropriate; offer ideas when students are at a loss for effective gestures and sound effects.

In the preliminary reading of the sample CBRT script, you will probably need to stop and restart so that students practice their lines, gestures, and sound effects on cue and in unison, when specified. At this point, you function much as a choral director does—standing in front of the group, directing, signaling, reading, and cueing sound effects and gestures. If you can, it's often helpful to students (even the older ones) when you "mirror" the gestures that they will perform. In other words, if students hold their scripts in their left hand and gesture with their right, you face them and hold your script in your right hand and gesture with your left.

It's most efficient to hold several read-throughs of the sample CBRT script. The first read-through of the sample script will be a stop-and-start experience. You and the students will need to decide upon and practice performing the gestures and sound effects on cue and in unison. Some students may fail to deliver a line on cue, while others may mispronounce words and need help with a **line reading**. A rough first read-through is quite normal.

The second read-through usually proceeds more smoothly. Two times through a sample script can be enough, but a third read-through shows remarkable and gratifying improvement in reading fluency and expression.

> **Read-Through:** An initial step in the play rehearsal process. The actors, who remain seated, read their lines aloud from the script. They read not to give a performance but, rather, to hear the script spoken and to begin to get ideas for vocal expression and other production elements.

> **Line Reading:** "The manner in which an actor delivers a line: the inflections, tone, volume, and pace used" (*NTC's Dictionary of Theatre and Drama Terms*, Mobley, 1995, p. 82).

Discussing the Sample CBRT Script With Students

After two or three read-throughs of a sample script, explain to students that the writers of the sample script had two goals: to inform and to entertain. Ask the students first to examine the script for evidence of how the writers tried to make it entertaining. Students' responses generally include observations about the incorporation of sound effects and gestures, the use of humor, slang, contemporary or conversational language, and opportunities for the participation of many speakers. Then, ask the students to examine the script for the content information it contains. Have them identify facts or ideas that the script presents.

This discussion's emphasis on the dual goals of writing for both purposes—entertaining and informing—is an important element of the CBRT process. The scripts that students create will also have to meet those two purposes. Chapter 3 details the next step in familiarizing students with CBRT—collaborating on an original CBRT script.

Collaborating With Students on an Original Script

How do you use the collaborative model to work with students to write and revise an original Curriculum-Based Readers Theatre script?

In writing a Curriculum-Based Readers Theatre (CBRT) script, students and teachers function as playwrights commissioned to write a script based on a topic they are studying in class. Their script has a dual purpose—it must inform as well as entertain. CBRT scripts can provide information about social studies topics like World War II, daily life in Japan, or transportation in ancient Rome. English grammar topics such as dangling modifiers and parts of speech may be scripted as CBRT. Math and science information can also be dramatized in this fashion: What distinguishes the three types of triangles? What is an improper fraction? What is a meteor? What is the composition of an atom? (See chapter 1, page 4, for other examples of CBRT script topics.)

However, before students can become independent CBRT scriptwriters, they must develop an understanding of the scriptwriting process. Therefore, the students' first original scriptwriting experience will be conducted with the collaborative script model—in collaboration with you, their teacher. Together, you and the students will work from a list of content area facts, agree upon a context for a CBRT script, write the script's opening lines, and read the script aloud as you continue creating it, adding gestures and sound effects and making edits.

As with most introductions to new ways of working, and as in the previous chapter, the process outlined in this chapter requires class time that will not be needed in subsequent uses of CBRT. Once the students have experienced and understand the CBRT writing process, the script creation proceeds quickly, and capable students can write scripts independently. However, Figure 6 provides a detailed list of the steps involved in your students' first exposure to writing a CBRT

FIGURE 6. Steps for Creating a Collaborative Model CBRT Script With Students

1. Choose a topic for the collaborative model script.
   - Narrow the script topic.
   - Limit the script length.

2. Create the first draft of the collaborative model script.
   - Identify the topic.
   - List information to include in the script.
   - Anticipate the audience.
   - Consider possible contexts and characters.
   - Write the opening lines.
   - Encourage students' script ideas.
   - Record the lines.
   - Develop the script.
   - Provide dialogue line-starters and other scriptwriting techniques.

3. Prepare the first draft for revision.

4. Revise the first draft.

5. Complete the final script.

script using the collaborative model. Each of the following steps, which will require two to three 50-minute class periods, pertain to your students' first exposure to writing a CBRT script: (1) choose a topic for a collaborative model script, (2) model the creation of a collaborative script, and (3) revise the collaborative model script.

Choosing a Topic for the Collaborative Model Script

When selecting a topic for the collaborative model script that you and the students will write, consider the enduring understandings of a unit of study and the processes or facts students need to be able to recall from memory. Examine your curriculum guides and standards of learning for facts that will appear on tests. Use your prior knowledge of the ideas and information that students find difficult to distinguish and recall. Any content area containing information that students are responsible for learning and retaining can provide the focus of the script. For example, procedures, strategies, terms, definitions, quotations, names, dates, or vocabulary can provide the informational component of a CBRT script.

Perhaps the information is the sort students should remember for the rest of their lives—multiplication facts, how germs are transmitted, the First Amendment to the United States Constitution, "*i* before *e* except after *c*," or the mathematical order of operations. Perhaps it's information they will be tested on—explorers of the New World, the Pythagorean theorem, figurative language, or parts of a cell. Consider the facts and specifics that will benefit your students if committed to their long-term memories.

Narrowing the Script Topic

A word of caution might help you avoid supersizing your scripts. Keep the focus of the CBRT script topic narrow: Halley's comet—not the solar system; the Middle Colonies—not Colonial America; Leonardo da Vinci—not the Renaissance. Too much information will lengthen the writing and editing process. It will result in a script that may be too long to rehearse and present effectively, thus sacrificing the interest of both performers and audience.

Limiting Script Length

For general classroom use, think in terms of a maximum script length of two typewritten pages. Scripts that fill no more than the front and back of a piece of paper are long enough to deliver the information and brief enough to keep the students' interest. An efficient way to keep within the two pages is to format the script in two columns. The additional benefit of a complete script on the front and back of one page becomes apparent later during rehearsals and performances. Rather than having to turn and flip stapled pages (think of the potential for noise and confusion here), students simply turn their papers over and continue the presentation.

Depending on your topic or purpose, scripts shorter than two pages can absolutely meet everyone's needs. More able and motivated students can certainly handle longer scripts. There are no absolute rules about script length. As with any learning activity, let your own teacher wisdom about your students and your topic guide your decision making.

SCRIPT SECTION: THE RENAISSANCE

1: [sound effect—trumpet fanfare]

2: Welcome to "Celebrities Select!"

All: [sound effect—applause, cheers]

3: The program that brings you celebrities from all time periods!

4: Even if they're dead!

All: [sound effect—admiration]

5: This week's guests come to us from the Renaissance!

1: Audience, do you know what the Renaissance is?

All: No, what does it mean?

2: It means a revival or rebirth of learning and culture.

3: Rebirth—what's that?

4: It means "coming alive a second time!"

All: Ohhhh! [gesture] Renaissance—a rebirth of learning and culture!

5: Anyways, the Renaissance went from the 1300s to the mid-1600s.

6: Many famous artists, inventors, musicians, and writers lived during that time.

All: Like who? [gesture]

7: Like Leonardo da Vinci,

8: Gutenberg,

9: Shakespeare,

10: Thomas More,

11: and Michelangelo!

1: Brought from the Renaissance right here to you today!

Creating the First Draft
of the Collaborative Model Script

In the theater, when a script is a collaborative project, the head playwright assembles and supervises a team of writers. Especially during the introductory phase of CBRT work, the teacher assumes the role of head playwright, modeling the creation of a script as part of the scaffolding process that will eventually lead to student independence with scriptwriting. When students are learning the CBRT process, you carefully guide them through the scriptwriting, helping them with format, accurate content, and distribution of lines. Once students are familiar with CBRT and able to write their own scripts, you retain a supervisory role to ensure that students' scripts meet criteria established for content and composition. As head playwright, you are "commissioning" this script and you retain the right to add or delete elements.

Identifying the Topic

As head playwright and teacher, you choose the collaborative CBRT script topic based on the content information you want to emphasize for your students. Inform the students of the topic and explain that together you and they will create a script to learn the CBRT scriptwriting process. If students' response to the topic is less than enthusiastic, remind them that one of their writing goals is to figure out how to script this information so that it is entertaining. Refer back to the sample script from chapter 2 on page 23 or 24 that you used to introduce CBRT. Examine its information and how the writers created entertaining ways to present that information.

The topic of the collaborative model script used as an example in this chapter is polygons.

Listing Information to Include in the Script

After identifying the topic of the model CBRT script, brainstorm with students the information that should be included in the script. If necessary, invite them to scrutinize their sources—examine the textbook chapter, reread the piece of literature, review the photocopied sheet. CBRT scripting can occur at the start of a unit of study, giving students a purpose for reading carefully, or it can cap off a unit whereby students recall and review what they have studied.

Create a list of the pieces of information generated by the students, feeling free to add anything important that they may have omitted. You may prompt or contribute ideas, make corrections or additions, and veto inappropriate elements. (*Note.* When time is a factor, you could create the list of script information yourself.)

It's a good idea to create the brainstormed list on pieces of chart paper that can be saved, rather than on a chalkboard where it can be erased. If your school has an interactive computer white board, using it for lists and scriptwriting will streamline the CBRT process.

So, for example, with a script topic of polygons, your list of information to include might look like Figure 7.

FIGURE 7. List of Information for Polygon CBRT Script

Polygon—a two-dimensional figure, a geometric shape on a plane
plane = flat surface
poly = many
gon = a figure with a specific number or kind of angles
All polygon sides are straight and closed.
3-sided polygon = triangle
4-sided polygons = square, rectangle, rhombus, trapezoid, parallelogram
5-sided polygon = pentagon
6-sided polygon = hexagon
8-sided polygon = octagon
A vertex is the point where two sides of a polygon meet.
Vertices = the plural for vertex.
Polygons have vertices.

Anticipating the Audience

CBRT challenges students to present accurate information in creative ways. Their script must be more than a dull recitation of facts. As playwrights, their goal is to create a script likely to evoke audience interest, so it cannot be boring. This stipulation provides students with opportunities to infuse their writing with humor, contemporary references and expressions, sarcasm, and other uses of language. With your students, determine the audience for your collaborative model CBRT script and keep this audience in mind as you write. Typically, the audience for these CBRT scripts is students who are in the same grade as the writers.

Because one intention of the script is to communicate appropriate curriculum content material, most CBRT scripts are aimed at an audience of students who will need to learn that material. If, however, the audience for your CBRT script will be younger students, parents, administrators, or another group of people, you may need to adjust the script's language, tone, humor, and references. During the writing phase, students and teachers may also begin to incorporate ideas for sound effects and gestures into the script, although many of those additions occur later when the students hear the words they have written read aloud.

Considering Possible Contexts and Characters

The next step requires some creative thinking about possible contexts for the script. For example, consider how the script might be framed to deliver the information. What might be an interesting way to present this collection of facts or description of a process? In what kind of circumstance might people or characters be hearing about, discussing, or presenting this information?

Pose the questions in the previous paragraph to students and solicit their ideas. The script's context might be a game show or talk show, an interview with characters or historical figures, or a scene from a mathematical mystery movie. It might take place in the cafeteria, the school hallway, a classroom, a courtroom, or a restaurant. If students need to jumpstart their "inner playwrights," share the chart of ideas in Figure 8 for possible CBRT contexts and characters.

In CBRT scripts, all speakers function essentially as narrators, but individual speakers can also play characters or historical figures. The following are additional roles speakers can play:

- someone in need of information
- someone who knows the information
- the doubter
- the joker or punster
- the enthusiast
- the clueless one
- an announcer or emcee

The most creative CBRT scripts have come from ideas about contexts and characters generated by students who were asked only to imagine the possibilities. Students would propose a few ideas; usually one suggestion would prompt a chorus of agreement from classmates and the decision would be made. If you or

FIGURE 8. Possible Contexts and Characters for CBRT Scripts

Contexts	Museum Tour	The Jokester
Auction	Press Conference	Jury/Judge
Awards Ceremony	Rally	The Know-It-All
"Beauty" Contest	Restaurant	Literary Characters
Boot Camp	Sporting Event	Military Officer
Campaign	Talk Show	Outraged Citizens
Cartoon	Tribute	Parents
Celebration	"You Are There"	Police Officer
Circus		Politicians
Classroom	**Characters**	Reporters
Commercial	Authors	Royalty
Court of Inquiry	Celebrity	Salesperson
Demonstration	Cheerleaders	Scientist
Department Store	Contestants	Spies
Documentary	Detectives	Sportscaster
Evening News	Doubters	Superhero
Fairy Tale	Enthusiasts	Teammates
Fashion Show	Gossip Columnist	Tour Guide
Game Show	Historians	Town Crier
Infomercial	Historical Figures	TV Personalities
Melodrama	Inventors	The Uninformed One

your students need a more structured approach, use one of the CBRT Templates in Appendix B of this book. Choose a template that will work for your topic and present the students with preestablished context, characters, and opening lines.

Writing the Opening Lines

Once you have agreed upon a context, ask students to suggest possible opening lines for their script. Encourage students to think creatively and avoid criticizing anyone's ideas. At this point, a good strategy for increasing the students' ownership of the script is to refrain from contributing your ideas for an opening line. Soliciting students' ideas often produces delightful, imaginative results—possibilities that probably would not have even occurred to you.

Listen to several suggested first lines; record some of them on chart paper or an overhead transparency. Keep in mind (and tell students) that the best first lines usually reveal the setting, context, or topic of the CBRT presentation. Think dramatically. Evoke interest. Perhaps begin with a question or exclamation such as the following:

- "Hello. You have reached the Homework Hotline. Press 1 for Math."
- "Ladies and Gentlemen! Boys and Girls! Let's give a warm welcome to The Polygon Patrol!"
- "Hey, did anyone do last night's homework?"
- "Live from the Geome, it's the Miss Polygon Pageant!"
- "Ugh! I have a huge test on polygons tomorrow!"

With the students, determine the opening lines in this first draft of the script and record them so that everyone can read them on chart paper or a computer white board. Remember that you have to begin somewhere, and every line can still be changed or replaced.

The first few lines are the most challenging ones to come up with. Once you have the script context and opening lines, continue seeking the students' suggestions for subsequent lines. You may need to keep reminding students that the purpose of their script is both to inform and entertain. They can have fun with the language, but they must be accurate with and include the facts. They also must remember that their audience will receive the information by listening, so their word choices and explanations matter. In your role as head playwright, you help shape and elevate the direction of the script.

SCRIPT SECTION: POLYGONS

| **1:** | Live from the world of math, it's the | **2:** | brought to you by |
| **All:** | "Love the Shape You're In" Beauty Pageant! [gesture] [sound effect] | **3:** | Polygon International, |

All: the company with all the angles! [gesture]	**8:** Tell our audience what that means.
4, 5: "All our sides are straight [gesture] [sound effect] and closed [gesture] [sound effect].	**All:** [gesture] Two-dimensional means you must be flat! [gesture] [sound effect]
All: Straight [gesture] [sound effect] and closed [gesture] [sound effect].	**9:** In other words—a plane!
6: Not just any shape is eligible to compete.	**10:** A plane? [airplane gesture]
7: All of our contestants must have	**11:** No—in the world of math, a plane means a flat surface [gesture].
All: [gesture] a two-dimensional figure.	**1:** To be eligible, you must be
	All: Plane and flat. [gesture]

Encouraging Students' Script Ideas

What often surprises and pleases students during this process is when you record a line that one of them just blurts out—perhaps it is an attempt to be funny, a contemporary slang phrase, or a sarcastic comment. If it could possibly fit, record and use it. In one middle school math class brainstorming ideas for a line at the start of their polygon script, a student joked, "Polly's gone?"

The line got a laugh and became a part of the script, providing an opportunity for both entertainment and a subsequent line giving the correct math term and its definition. The teaching challenge at this point of the CBRT process is to remain open to students' ideas, language, humor, and playfulness while still guiding them to fulfill both writing purposes—informing and entertaining.

Recording the Lines

During this initial scriptwriting, record several lines but do not yet assign numbers to indicate speakers. The following section of the polygon script illustrates what the script will look like at this stage, when lines have not yet been assigned.

[TV news bulletin sound effect] We interrupt this program to bring you an important news bulletin. A two-dimensional figure was just spotted hovering over City Hall.	Live footage from the scene. Oh no! Not a polygon! Oh yes! [gesture] A closed geometric shape with many sides!

After you and the students have created five to eight lines, go back and assign solo or group speakers to each line. When you assign lines to speakers, keep the following points in mind:

- To motivate attentive reading and whole-group involvement, seek to give as many lines as possible to "All."

- Because it is difficult for a group of speakers to come in together on the first line, give the first line to a solo speaker.

- To allow for a large number of solo speaking parts, avoid having just one narrator, emcee, or reporter. Divide those lines among as many solo speakers as possible.

- To maximize the number of solo speakers, keep each line relatively short. Divide sentences, if necessary, so that one speaker finishes a sentence or question begun by another speaker.

- If struggling readers, English-language learners, or shy students would benefit from sharing lines with others, assign lines to pairs or small groups.

Once you start assigning speakers to the lines with numbers or "All," the script begins to take form. At this stage, your script should resemble the following example.

1:	[sound effect—TV news bulletin]	**2, 3:**	Live footage from the scene.
2:	We interrupt this program to bring you an important news bulletin.	**4:**	Oh no! Not a polygon!
3:	A two-dimensional figure was just spotted hovering over City Hall.	**All:**	Oh yes! [gesture] A closed geometric shape with many sides!

Developing the Scripts

Assign the lines written thus far to students and read through the beginning of the script. Make adjustments, add gestures and sound effects, and then read through the script again. As you add the next five or six lines, indicate which ones are to be spoken by "All." Then assign solo speakers to the new lines and read through the script from the beginning. Add more lines, indicate speakers, add gestures and sound effects, and keep on going back to the beginning to read through the script. Continue to follow this process, always re-harnessing students' attention by returning to the beginning of the script and rereading aloud as much as you have written.

There are a variety of ways to fully develop and complete the first draft of the script. You may continue in your role as head playwright and complete the writing as a whole-class activity. Students as young as second graders can participate in CBRT, but younger and less able students rely more on the teacher to develop the script using their ideas.

However, with older and more capable students who can assume writing responsibilities, you may give the start of the collaborative model script to a small group of students who work together to complete it. You may assign several small groups portions of information (several facts or a paragraph or two from a text, for example) and let them create the first draft for that section of the script. The polygon information in Figure 7 (see page 30) could be distributed so that one group writes a script portion on pentagons, another group is responsible for the hexagon script portion, and other groups write about octagons and vertices.

Your decision on how to proceed is, of course, determined by the ability and enthusiasm of the students involved. As long as the script accurately contains the necessary information, students can be as imaginative as they wish in creating characters, dialogue, and context.

SCRIPT SECTION: POLYGONS

1: Hello. What kind of house are you looking for?

2–4: We need a quadrilateral.

5–7: We are looking for a hexagon.

8–10: We are interested in your octagon model.

11: Well, you've come to the right place!

1: Polygon Palace!

All: [sung] Polygon Palace! Polygon Palace! [gesture]

If you want a home with a vertex, a vertex,
you're going to live in great shape, great shape! [gesture]

2: Remind me again—what's a vertex?

3: A vertex is the point where two sides of a polygon meet, remember?

4: Like a sharp corner, remember?

2: Oh, yeah!

Providing Dialogue Line-Starters and Other Scriptwriting Techniques

One challenge students face in writing CBRT scripts is creating lines that lead into lines that give information. If your students need help coming up with ways to start lines of dialogue in their script, posting the list in Figure 9 might give them some ideas. Other scriptwriting techniques you and your students may want to use include chants; incorrect responses that are corrected by another speaker; repeated words, phrases, or gestures; call and response; rhyming and alliteration; words sung to a familiar melody; or a tune hummed underneath spoken words. These techniques have the potential to add variety, humor, and perhaps a theatrical touch to CBRT scripts. Making students aware of a variety of scriptwriting ideas often jumpstarts their thinking and creativity, thus enlivening both their script and their enthusiasm for writing it. The examples on pages 36 and 37 illustrate some of these creative scriptwriting techniques.

FIGURE 9. Dialogue Line-Starters

If your students need help coming up with ways to start lines of dialogue that lead to providing curriculum information in their script, posting this list might give them some ideas.

What's _____?

What do you mean by _____?

Remember when/how _____?

In other words, _____.

How about _____?

Why do you say _____?

Not only that, but _____.

And what about _____?

Can you believe _____?

You mean _____?

Oh, I get it—_____.

Isn't it true that _____?

Yeah, but _____.

Do you know what _____ means?

Have you ever heard of _____?

Why do you say _____?

CHANTS

All:	Range—the distance between two numbers!	Range—the distance from the greatest to the least!

INCORRECT RESPONSES THAT ARE CORRECTED BY ANOTHER SPEAKER

1:	OK, what are the five elements of a story?	**2:**	Psych. The five elements of a story are setting, characters, point of view, plot, and theme.
All:	Wind, water, fire, earth, and...		
1:	C'mon you guys!		

REPEATED WORDS, PHRASES, OR GESTURES

1:	Poe was fascinated with death and horror.	**3:**	revenge and guilt,
All:	Death and horror! [gesture]	**4:**	insanity and lost love.
2:	His most famous writings were about death,	**All:**	Death, revenge, guilt, insanity, and lost love.

CALL AND RESPONSE

1:	Prefixes first!	**All:**	*de*—take away; *pre*—before.
2:	*im*, *dis*, and *un* all mean *not*.	**4:**	*sub*—under and below.
All:	*im*, *dis*, and *un* all mean *not*.	**All:**	*sub*—under and below!
3:	*de*—take away; *pre*—before.		

RHYMING AND ALLITERATION

All: In search of routes and riches, / To unknown lands they came.

They've earned themselves a place / in the Explorers Hall of Fame!

WORDS SUNG TO A FAMILIAR MELODY

1: Where do you live?

All: [sung] In the jungle, the Mexican jungle, the Olmec sleep each night. [to the tune of "The Lion Sleeps Tonight," recorded by The Tokens and written by Solomon Linda, George David Weiss, Hugo Peretti, and Luigi Creatore]

TUNE HUMMED UNDERNEATH SPOKEN WORDS

1: November 11, 1918.

All: [begin and continue humming "When Johnny Comes Marching Home"]

2: The setting—5:00 a.m. in a railroad car parked in a French forest near the front lines.

3: The Germans and Allies agree to end World War I

4: precisely at the 11th hour of the 11th day of the 11th month.

5: They sign an armistice—

1–4: *Armistice*—a temporary suspension of fighting as a prelude to peace negotiations.

5: After more than four years of bloody conflict, the Great War—

1: the war to end all wars—

5: was over.

If at the end of this step in the CBRT writing process you find yourself with a questionable collection of words, lines, and pieces of paper, you are definitely on the right track! The next portion of this chapter will help you and your students work with the first draft, refine the CBRT script, and make it more theatrical.

SCRIPT SECTION: SCIENTIFIC METHOD

1: Welcome to Science Fair Boot Camp!

2: For the next two weeks, you will learn how to do your Science Fair project.

1: First, you need a science problem.

2: What comes first?

All: The science problem, sir!

2: Right! The scientific problem to be solved!

3: Next, you must make an educated guess about your outcome!

4: What is this educated guess called?

All: Hypothesis, sir!

4: Hypothesis! Correct!

3: You also need materials!

4: in a list!

All: Materials list! Check!

1: Who knows what comes next?

5: Conclusion!

1: Wrong! Drop and give me 20!

6: [laughs at 5]

2:	You think it's funny?	**All:**	procedures, sir!
6:	Uhhhh...	**1:**	Correct! The steps in your project!
2:	Drop and give me 20!	**All:**	[marching] Step by step! Step by
3:	The accurate answer is		step!

Preparing the First Draft for Revision

The collaborative model CBRT script's first draft—the copy the students will receive and read through as a group—is pulled together by the teacher. Once students are familiar with CBRT, they may assume complete responsibility for all drafts of the script, but initially (especially if this is an activity for a whole class or a large group), you are modeling the process. As head playwright, your job is to work with the students' writing and return it to them in script form with blanks and options for revisions. Therefore, you collect the writing and type up the first draft. This involves transferring the lines from the collaborative model script and from the students' section drafts (if applicable) to a computer word-processing program. (More detailed information on computer formatting the CBRT script is provided in Appendix C.)

As much as possible, use the students' words. However, when you type the script, consider potential areas of improvement. Even though it is important to retain appropriate and effective contributions from the students' independent work, you should discard inappropriate and repetitive ones. Format and type up the script, indicating speakers by numbers. Assign preliminary numbers that indicate speakers of the lines of dialogue (preliminary because these numbers may later be changed). Assign lines to individuals, pairs, small groups, and the whole group ("All"). Build volume by adding several voices line by line, as in the following example.

11:	But we still have to conserve the energy we have today...	**1–5:**	clean,
12:	and keep searching for and developing energy sources that are	**1–10:**	renewable,
		1–18:	inexpensive,
		1–25:	and dependable!

Because the accurate comprehension and retention of content information is one of the most important goals of CBRT, you should also scrutinize the script's first draft for places where information is missing or stated unclearly. It is helpful to insert blank lines where additional information or explanations would strengthen the script in order to prompt students to supply this information. It is also helpful to use italics to pose questions that will prompt students' thinking and increase the quality of the script and to offer ideas for line recommendations. During the first script read-through, the students can make decisions about how to fill in any blank lines and address the other ideas indicated in italics.

To enhance the clarity and entertainment value of the script, it is a good idea to help smooth out transitions. One way to do this is by changing a statement to a question—"Paul Revere rode at midnight," for example, becomes "In what year did Paul Revere ride at midnight?" and sets up for subsequent lines to communicate more information. Repeating important words or phrases also helps serve this purpose. For example, the following script section illustrates the transformation of the line "Equilateral triangles have sides and angles that are congruent."

1:	Equilateral triangles have sides and angles that are congruent.	**3:**	*Congruent* means "the same."
2:	*Congruent*?	**All:**	*Congruent* means "the same."

Adding lines that ask for clarification of a previous line—such as "What do you mean?" "What's that?" or "Can you run that by me again?"—can also serve as a transition.

When preparing the script, also look for or create lines that the entire group—"All"—can speak together. (The more lines assigned to "All," the more every student participates in the reading.) Lines spoken by "All" may simply be the repetition of a previous line or a word or phrase of reaction—for example, "Cool!" "Sounds strange." "Ohhhh, now we get it!" or "Whatever!" It is most effective, however, for "All" to speak lines containing definitions or facts worth remembering, such as in the following example.

7:	When a comet breaks up, its little pieces are called meteoroids.	**All:**	Meteoroids—broken-up comet pieces! [sound effect] [gesture]
8:	Meteoroids?		

If the students identified places where gestures or sound effects might occur, insert the stage direction [gesture] or [sound effect]. Likewise, if you notice places where gestures or sound effects would emphasize the spoken words, insert the stage directions in brackets within the script.

Moreover, do not forget to think theatrically: What might help this script become more dynamic, more interesting to perform and to watch? Refer to the scriptwriting techniques recommended on page 35 of this chapter for ideas.

The first draft of your CBRT script may give concrete meaning to the term *rough draft*. It may look extremely sketchy, contain several errors and numerous blank lines, read only barely like a script, and need lots of revision. Because the first draft is always edited, you may also want to record even inaccurate wording, spelling, and facts because you and the students will correct and revise the script during the first read-through. This way, students can see their errors, and this step in the CBRT process serves as an excellent demonstration of how revisions improve writing.

Once the first draft of the collaborative model CBRT script is prepared, make photocopies for the class. When you assemble and type up the students' contributions to the script as described, the first draft you give them may look like the following sample.

1: [TV news bulletin sound effect]

2: We interrupt this program to bring you an important news bulletin.

3: A two-dimensional figure was just spotted hovering over City Hall.

2, 3: Live footage from the scene.

4: Oh no! Not a polygon!

All: Oh yes! [gesture] A closed geometric shape with many sides!

5: What could it be? (*Is this a reporter talking?*)

6: It's a three-sided figure! (*Could this be an eyewitness kind of character?*)

7: Could it be a triangle?

8: Are all three sides straight?

9: Yes.

10: Are all three sides closed?

11: Yes.

12: Is it on a plane? (*You mean an airplane?*)

13: No, it is flying all by itself!

All: Oh, no it's not! Look everyone! (*Look where?*)

14: The triangle has some company.

15: A square, a rectangle, a rhombus, a trapezoid, and a parallelogram! (*Split these up—one polygon per speaker?*)

16: What in the world are they?

17: Those are the names of polygons that have four sides.

18: What do you call a five-sided polygon?

19: A five-o-gon?

All: [sound effect] No—a pentagon!

20: Like the building in Washington, DC, they always talk about on the news?

(*Opportunity for calling on the Pentagon in this emergency situation?*)

All: Right! [gesture]

1: I wonder why they didn't name it The Hexagon....

2: Because the Pentagon has five sides, not six _____

(*Need more hexagon info.*)

_____

_____

3: Do you see any hexagons up there over City Hall?

4: No, but what's that?

6: Look, Mommy—there's an eight-sided figure! [gesture]

All: An octagon? [sound effect]

7: Where, Junior?

6: On top of that pole. It's red! Stop! [gesture]

7: Stop what!

8: Ohhhh—he means the stop sign!

All: Oh right—a stop sign is an octagon.

6: It has eight sides and eight points.

All: A point of a polygon is called a vertex.

11: (*Insert a "clueless" type of line—something about vertexes here.*)

All: And the plural of vertex is vertices!

9: (*Repeat vertices definition.*)

(*Needs an ending to wrap things up.*)

_____

_____

_____

_____

Revising the First Draft

Hand out the photocopied first draft of the script to students for the initial read-through. Distribute photocopies, assign numbered lines to speakers, and begin reading the script aloud. It's helpful to remind students that the lines they read at this point may not be their lines in the final performance—the purpose of this read-through is for everyone to hear the words spoken. Hearing the written words helps students recognize inconsistencies, omissions, and imprecise language.

Solicit students' ideas for filling in the blanks and record their responses on your copy of the first draft. Encourage them to search through dictionaries, textbooks, or other reference material for necessary information. Encourage them to think theatrically: "How can we enhance this script to hold an audience's attention?" "How can we grab them and make them want to watch and listen?" Encourage them to add humor, if appropriate. Encourage the use of contemporary language or slang, if it suits the topic or audience. (Words like *hot*, *totally*, *whatever*, *dude*, *awesome*, *duh*, for example, were in common use when this book was written.) Let students see that they have an enormous amount of freedom to shape the script, as long as they remember their dual purpose: creating a script that both informs and entertains.

Your teaching role in this phase of the script creation is truly that of facilitator. When students are given this type of artistic freedom, the dialogue and ideas that they come up with can be amazing. You help them by encouraging their creativity, allowing them to insert contemporary language, and accepting appropriate humorous or unusual contributions. You also serve as the moderator who keeps them accurate; focused; and within the boundaries of language, references, and gestures suitable for a classroom activity. Always remember (and remind students) that as supervising or head playwright, you retain veto rights over any portion of the script.

Completing the Final Script

Using the notes you made during the read-through of the first draft, make the changes that result in the next draft. Return to the first draft of the CBRT script on your computer. Insert the changes that you and your students agreed upon and

CBRT IN ACTION

I had just finished a CBRT classroom modeling session in which I had collaborated with ninth-grade students on revising the first draft of their script and adding gestures and sound effects. After the session, their teacher expressed sentiments similar to those of many teachers I have worked with, explaining why he found it helpful to observe the process: "Given the exuberant nature of these idea-filled students, it was good for me to watch you manage their creativity. It was clearly necessary for you to make definite choices about the gestures and sound effects and other performance elements and keep the work moving forward. Otherwise, with so many students offering ideas and trying to insist that their ideas were the best ones to use, you would not have gotten through the script. Watching you work in that way gives me permission to allow creativity within boundaries."

format the script. Consult Appendix C on page 101 for specific guidelines on computer formatting the CBRT script. As with any piece of writing, the final draft of a CBRT script could be revised again and again. That is what happens to scripts in the professional theater, but in classrooms there's generally not enough time for that kind of attention to detail. In order to move beyond the writing and into the rehearsing and performing, this second draft usually becomes the final draft of the script.

One major piece of information you will need before creating the final draft is the number of solo speakers in the script. As the teacher, you may stipulate that each student speak at least one solo line. If you wish to allow students the choice of speaking solo, ask for a show of hands and count the number of solo speakers to write into the final draft. If your class is large, you can usually adjust the script to accommodate every student who wants to speak solo—even if that means only one line per student. Because CBRT scripts call for the frequent use of all students speaking in unison, those students who do not choose to speak lines alone are still heavily involved in the reading and oral delivery of the script.

CBRT IN ACTION

The eighth graders had written and rehearsed a social studies CBRT script on representation in Congress. Twenty of the 25 students had requested solo parts. On the day of the first performance, one of the solo speakers was absent. The teacher and I asked the students whether any of them would be willing to perform the lines of the absent student. Lots of hands shot up. One of the volunteers was a boy new to the United States whose English was limited. He had previously chosen not to speak any solo lines. Because he had repeatedly rehearsed the script, speaking the unison lines and hearing the solo lines, he now felt confident enough to speak alone. The teacher chose this boy to speak the solo lines—which he delivered beautifully, resulting in many compliments from his classmates.

After revising the first draft of the polygons script, you and your students might produce a final draft for 20 solo speakers that looks like the following script. (See Appendix A, page 87, for a reproducible version of this script.)

POLYGON NEWSCAST

By Rosalind M. Flynn

1: [TV news bulletin sound effect]

2: We interrupt this program to bring you an important news bulletin.

3: A two-dimensional figure was just spotted hovering over City Hall.

2, 3: Live footage from the scene.

4: Oh no! Not a polygon!

All: Oh yes! [gesture] A closed geometric shape with many sides!

5: Please, someone—tell us what you see!

6: Look, Mommy—there's a three-sided figure! [gesture]

7: Junior—don't look directly at it! It's a triangle!

All: [sound effect] It's a one- [gesture], it's a two- [gesture], it's a three- [gesture] sided polygon! A triangle!

8: Are all three sides straight? [gesture]

All: Straight! [gesture]

9: Are all three sides closed? [gesture]

All: Closed! [gesture]

10: Is the triangle on a plane?

11: No, it appears to be flying all by itself!

12: She didn't mean an airplane, dude!

All: In geometry, a plane is a flat surface. [gesture]

11: Right—plane...flat surface, man.

13: Look up again, everyone! [gesture] The triangle has some company.

14: It's a square!

15: It's a rectangle!

16: It's a rhombus!

17: It's a trapezoid!

18: It's a parallelogram!

All: It's the four-sided polygons [gesture]— squares, rectangles, rhombuses, trapezoids, and parallelograms!

19: Someone better alert the Pentagon!

All: Pentagon—a five-sided polygon.

20: Like the building in Washington, DC, they always talk about on the news?

All: Right! [gesture]

5: Who's got a cell phone?

All: I do. [gesture] [overlapping talking] Who knows the number? Can I text the Pentagon? Do they have caller ID?

11: I wonder why they didn't name it the Hexagon....

12: Duh—because the Pentagon has five sides and a hexagon has six sides.

6: Look, Mommy—there's an eight-sided figure! [gesture]

All: Eight-sided figure? An octagon? [sound effect]

7: Where's the octagon, Junior?

6: On top of that pole. It's red and it's telling me something!

All: [sound effect] What's it saying?

6: Stop! [gesture]

7: No, no, Junior! We need to know!

8: Ohhhh—he means the stop sign!

All: Oh right—a stop sign is an octagon.

6: It has eight sides and eight corners.

All: A corner of a polygon is called a vertex.

11: So, young man, your octagon has eight vertexes.

All: Not vertexes! Vertices! The plural of vertex is vertices!

9: Vertices—the points where the sides of the polygon meet.

10: Quiet everyone—she has the Pentagon on the phone right now!

All: [gesture—leaning in to listen]

13: What do they say about the polygons?

14: They say not to be alarmed. Polygons are harmless, and they're everywhere. Just look around you.

All: [sound effect] [gesture]

1: This is Polly Gonzalez with News Three-Plus signing off.

2, 3: We return you to your regularly scheduled program.

Creating a collaborative model CBRT script may serve as the teaching strategy to familiarize students with the CBRT script creation process, or it may be the only way that you can involve younger or less capable students in writing a script. Some students may continually need the support of a teacher to achieve script writing goals. Once they are familiar with CBRT, however, capable and motivated students can write scripts without the teacher functioning as head playwright. The next chapter contains information on how to involve students in the independent writing, revision, and assessment of CBRT scripts.

Involving Students
in Independent Scriptwriting

*How do you involve students in creating
and assessing their own original scripts?*

Once students are familiar with the Curriculum-Based Readers Theatre (CBRT) scriptwriting process, those who are capable can advance to writing CBRT scripts independently. CBRT is an excellent addition to any differentiated instruction repertoire, as discussed in chapter 1. Capable and motivated students can create scripts for a small group or the whole class to perform. In order to help students achieve more productive work sessions and higher quality scripts when undertaking independent scriptwriting, it is necessary to provide them with guidelines and procedures for this task.

Establishing Guidelines for Independent Student Scriptwriting

During this phase of CBRT work, you function in your traditional role of teacher, facilitating and establishing guidelines for student work. When students understand the criteria for excellence in the CBRT scripts that they will write, they overwhelmingly produce higher quality scripts. It is best not to assume that students remember or are aware of the elements that contribute to the effective scripts that they have previously read or collaborated on with the teacher as head playwright. Providing them with written guidelines in the form of a CBRT script planning sheet and a CBRT script assessment checklist increases the likelihood that their scripts will be well-written.

CBRT Script Planning Sheet

When you first assign students the scriptwriting task, it is important to provide them with a script planning sheet. The reproducible CBRT Script Planning Sheet on page 46 illustrates the general guidelines students should be equipped with as they begin scriptwriting. Note that the section marked "The CBRT script must inform the audience about all of the following" is where you can clearly communicate any content information or standards you want the script to address. The script planning sheet also reminds students to consider the audience for their CBRT script and identifies sources of information to consult for facts to include. You may use the planning sheet to direct students to include specific vocabulary words, direct quotes, names, dates, definitions, explanations, and examples as they write. On the planning sheet, you can also stipulate the number of solo lines and lines to be spoken by "All," the number of stage directions for gestures, sound effects, and the length of the written script. (Remember also that students may use one of the CBRT templates in Appendix B of this book to jumpstart their scriptwriting with preestablished context, characters, and opening lines.)

As an example of what a completed form should look like, Figure 10 is a sample planning sheet that specifies the criteria for a CBRT script on the science topic of saturated solutions.

SCRIPT SECTION: SATURATED SOLUTIONS

1:	Want some lemonade?	**Evens:**	Solution? Solute? Solvent? [gesture]
2:	Sure. Just mix that powder with the water.	**4:**	What in the world are they?
1:	[gesture] [sound effect]	**7:**	A solution is when a solid dissolves into a liquid.
Evens:	What's all that nasty stuff in the bottom of the pitcher? [sound effect]	**6:**	Oh I get it—like the ocean.
		8:	Or sugar stirred into coffee.
3:	Pardon me, but your solution is obviously saturated.	**Evens:**	Or like our lemonade! [gesture]
		5:	Exactly!
Evens:	Huh? English please!	**Odds:**	Precisely. [gesture]
5:	A solution is composed of a solute that has dissolved into a solvent.		

CBRT Script Assessment Checklist

One product of CBRT is a finished script that must fulfill a number of curriculum content, writing, speaking, and theatrical goals. (*Note.* The script can also be used repeatedly with future classes studying the same topic, or as a model for the creation of a new script.) CBRT scripts offer students opportunities to try different writing approaches and styles to demonstrate their comprehension of a topic, but there are a number of elements common to effective CBRT scripts. The goal of the

CBRT Script Planning Sheet

Scriptwriters _____

Topic of the CBRT script _____

Audience _____

Source(s) of information: _____

The CBRT script must inform the audience about all of the following:

_____

_____

_____

_____

_____

_____

_____

_____

_____

_____

_____

_____

The script should also include: ___ Specific vocabulary words ___ Direct quotes

___ Names ____ Dates ____ Definitions ___ Explanations ___ Examples

The CBRT script must contain:

_____ Solo lines for _____ speakers

_____ At least _____ lines for ALL speakers

_____ At least _____ stage directions for [gesture]

_____ At least _____ stage directions for [sound effect]

The CBRT script must NOT contain:

* "Blocking"—the theater term for stage movement (e.g., entrances, exits, stage positions)

* Separate scenes

Note. The written script should be between three and four pages long. The typed script should be no longer than two pages.

assessment checklist is to guide the creation of a CBRT script. It was developed to help make CBRT assessment simple and informative.

When students understand the assessment criteria prior to beginning a task, their learning and performance are enhanced (Arter & McTighe, 2001). When the characteristics of an excellent CBRT script are explicit from the start, students

FIGURE 10. Sample CBRT Script Planning Sheet

Scriptwriters _Amanda, Briona, William, and Chris_

Topic of the CBRT script _Saturated Solutions_

Audience _Middle School Students_

Source(s) of information: _Your science textbook_

The CBRT script must inform the audience about all of the following:

Saturated Solutions

Define and explain the following scientific terms:

　　　Solution

　　　Solute

　　　Solvent

　　　Saturated

Give examples of:

　　　Solution

　　　Solute

　　　Solvent

　　　Saturated

The script should also include: ____ Specific vocabulary words ____ Direct quotes

____ Names ____ Dates _X_ Definitions _X_ Explanations _X_ Examples

The CBRT script must contain:

_X_ Solo lines for _10_ speakers

_X_ At least _12_ lines for ALL speakers

_X_ At least _5_ stage directions for [gesture]

_X_ At least _5_ stage directions for [sound effect]

The CBRT script must NOT contain:
* "Blocking"—the theater term for stage movement (e.g., entrances, exits, stage positions)
* Separate scenes

Note. The written script should be between three and four pages long. The typed script should be no longer than two pages.

overwhelmingly produce higher quality scripts. Students are aware of the elements that their scripts must include and what they must do to succeed at this writing task. Explicit assessment tools aid teachers in motivating and assessing students' work, and students may use the tools to assess their own work and that of their peers.

What are the characteristics of an excellent CBRT script? To focus students on CBRT scriptwriting goals, communicate the assessment evidence that indicates that they have created or contributed to an effective written script. A reproducible CBRT Script Assessment Checklist has been included on page 49. To clarify scriptwriting goals, photocopy and distribute this checklist to students before they begin writing their CBRT scripts.

Content. The "Content" category concerns the script's content area information that must be learned as part of the curriculum. Inform students that you will be assessing the following elements of the script's content:

- To what extent is the curriculum or content information covered in the script? How well are the specified learning standards addressed in the script?
- How thoroughly does the script include all specified content elements such as facts, procedures, strategies, terms, names, dates, definitions, direct quotations, original language, and vocabulary?
- How accurately, effectively, and clearly does the script communicate the content information? Is there sufficient detail?

Mechanics. The "Mechanics" category focuses on the functional aspects of the script—speakers, sound effects, gestures, spelling, and appearance of the script copy. Let students know that you will be looking for the following:

- To what extent does the script contain parts for the specified number of speakers?
- To what extent does the script include a variety of solo lines and lines that are spoken by the whole group, by small groups, and by pairs?
- To what extent does the script include stage directions for sound effects?
- To what extent does the script include stage directions for gestures?
- To what extent is the spelling correct?
- How legible is the script? Is it neatly written or typed?

Style. The "Style" category deals with the script's distinctive features and manner of expression. Inform students that you will be observing the following:

- How effectively do the script's opening lines establish the script's context—set the scene—and grab the audience's attention?
- To what extent are the script's language and word choices effective and appropriate for its intended audience?

CBRT Script Assessment Checklist

Script Topic or Title: _____

Script Writer(s): _____

	Strong 3	Adequate 2	Minimal 1	No Evidence 0
CONTENT				
All required **content information** (e.g., dates, vocabulary, definitions) is **included**.				
Content information is **accurate**.				
Content information is clearly and effectively **communicated**.				
MECHANICS				
There are **solo speaking parts** for the specified number (___) of speakers.				
Lines are distributed among solo, pair, small-group, and whole-group voices.				
Opportunities for **sound effects** are created and indicated in stage directions.				
Opportunities for **gestures** are created and indicated in stage directions.				
Spelling is accurate.				
Script is **legible**.				
STYLE				
Opening lines capture the audience's attention.				
Language is effective and appropriate for intended audience.				
Overall **context** of script remains consistent throughout the text.				
Script contains **entertaining** elements.				
Closing is logical and effective.				

Total out of 42 _____

- To what extent is the chosen context of the script apparent and effective? How well is the context maintained throughout the text of the script?

- To what extent does the script contain elements that make it entertaining as well as informative? Does the script show evidence of imagination, invention, or creativity? For example, the script may include the following:

  humor

  interesting characters

  a compelling context

  chants

  contemporary language

  repeated words, phrases, or gestures

  call and response

  rhyming and alliteration

  incorrect responses that are then corrected

  words sung to a familiar melody

  a tune hummed underneath spoken words

- How logical and effective is the script's closing—its final lines?

SCRIPT SECTION: CONFLICT IN LITERATURE

1:	What did you say, man?		**5:**	or disagreement or fighting.
2:	I said I don't like the way you're looking at me.		**6:**	We learned all about it in English class, right everyone?
1:	Oh yeah?		**All:**	Right! In literature, conflict is the struggle between two opposing forces. [gesture]
2:	Yeah!			
1:	Well, what are you going to do about it?		**7:**	There are five types of conflict.
2:	I'm going to...		**1:**	What type is ours?
3:	[interrupting] Oh! I believe you two are having a conflict!		**8:**	I would say Character vs. Character, wouldn't you?
1, 2:	A what? [gesture]		**All:**	Ummm hmmmm. [gesture]
4:	A conflict—it's a problem...			

Assessing the CBRT Script

The assessment checklist allows each element of a CBRT script to be assessed in varying degrees. The columns to the right of each listed element contain labels to note variations in students' levels of scriptwriting proficiency—meaning "Is this element of the script strong, adequate, minimal, or is there no evidence of it?" The following descriptions explain each of these rating labels:

Strong: This element's incorporation into the script is readily noticeable, complete, explicit, and forthright. It is intense in degree, quality, and condition—solid, sure, and firm.

Adequate: This element is present in the script and reflects the average or expected. This element is sufficient to satisfy a requirement or meet a need. It is acceptable and satisfactory but not outstanding.

Minimal: This element appears in the script in only the smallest amount or degree. It is only barely sufficient, constituting the least possible use with respect to size, number, degree, or stated goals.

No Evidence: This element is completely missing from the written script.

You may use the CBRT Script Assessment Checklist (see page 49) as is or adapt it to the specific needs of your students and curriculum goals. To convert the elements of the checklist into a numerical grade, you may use the suggested points assigned to each element category. Point allotments range from 3 for a determination of "strong" to 0 for "no evidence." Adding up the points per element will result in a total performance score.

SCRIPT SECTION: REPRESENTATION IN CONGRESS

All: [begin mumbling]

5: Order! [pause] The Philadelphia Constitutional Convention of 1787 is called to order.

11: It seems we've come to a standstill. We cannot agree about representation in Congress.

1: We the people of Virginia want more representatives! [gesture]

3: Because states with more people should have more representatives in Congress!

Odds: Aye! [gesture]

Evens: Nay! [gesture]

2: I'm from Delaware. We came to this country so we could have representation in how our laws are made.

4: If the bigger states have more representation, they'll have all the power!

Evens: Hear! Hear! [gesture]

Odds: [sound effect—grumbling]

7: The quality of representatives is more important than the quantity!

9: Therefore, send your best men and don't worry!

12: But the more votes a state has, the more power in Congress!

Odds: You're too small to matter anyway!

Evens: [sound effect] [gesture] Are you trying to say that our people don't matter?

Odds: The more people, the more representation! [gesture]

Evens: Each state should have the same number of representatives! [gesture]

All: [grumbling and chatter...]

5: Gentlemen! [pause for quiet] You are acting uncivilized!

Providing Instructions
for Small-Group CBRT Scriptwriting

Divide students into small groups to collaborate on CBRT scripts. Groups of two to four students generally work best because too many different opinions can slow the scriptwriting. Most scriptwriting begins with pencil and paper, but if computers are available, students may certainly compose directly into a word-processing program. While students work in groups, you may circulate among them, monitoring time and progress and offering ideas when needed. Whereas there are no hard and fast rules, the following instructions to students may be helpful:

1. Assemble with your group and discuss your script's curriculum topic.

2. Review the CBRT Script Planning Sheet. Be sure you understand all its requirements.

3. Research and make a list of all the information that your script must include, such as definitions, facts, and examples.

4. Decide on the context—the circumstances or setting—and characters for your script. For example, will it be a TV show, a press conference, a contest, or a commercial? You may create your own context and characters or use one of the CBRT templates.

5. Choose a scribe—a person to do the writing—and write your script.

   • Use pencil.

   • Use only one side of the paper. Number your pages.

   • For ease in making changes, begin by writing on every other line of the page or leaving blank lines between each speaker's lines of dialogue. That way, you have writing space if you decide to add any new lines, sound effects, or gestures.

   (Hint: You may want to write four or five lines without assigning speakers and then go back and indicate speakers by number. Then write the next four or five lines, stop, and go back and indicate speakers by number, and so on throughout the scriptwriting.)

6. Read your script aloud every so often to hear how it sounds.

7. Consult the CBRT Script Assessment Checklist to review the criteria for excellence in CBRT scripts.

8. If possible, type your script on the computer. (*Note.* You may need to turn off the AutoFormat that creates automatic numbered lists.)

9. Give your finished draft to the teacher for photocopying.

When the final draft of any CBRT script is completed, the focus of your work shifts to more theatrical concerns. The next chapter addresses the teacher's role as director in the rehearsals and performances of original CBRT scripts.

CHAPTER 5

Staging a Curriculum-Based Readers Theatre Performance

How do you rehearse for, present, and assess Curriculum-Based Readers Theatre performances?

The theatrical aspects of Curriculum-Based Readers Theatre (CBRT) provide students with a genuine purpose for the oral repetition of content material that might otherwise be tedious. The motivation of preparing for a performance—the artistic decision making involved and the recognition of the need to "get it right"—seems to elevate the work beyond rote repetition and validate the effort put into rehearsals. Many teachers will find that the CBRT work of writing and reading the content-based script aloud in class fulfills their curriculum and reading goals and objectives. Teachers who wish to take their students to the next level and mine the motivational aspects of performing for an audience will find guidance in the following pages. No prior theatrical directing experience is necessary!

This chapter will deepen your understanding of how to lead students through productive CBRT rehearsals, coach them in a variety of performance skills, provide them with the language and the focus for assessment, and prepare them to present their work for an audience. As you read, remember that the scope of a CBRT performance is up to your discretion. Some classes rehearse to perform only once for the class next door; other classes travel from classroom to classroom performing their script multiple times; others present their CBRT script at a school or evening assembly. Consider your CBRT performance goals and use the information in this chapter accordingly.

Introducing the Theatrical Components of CBRT

CBRT's arts-integrated focus becomes more sharpened when teachers and students work to stage the words on the page. The theatrical components of CBRT, like many speaking and listening curriculum objectives, involve students in using their voices effectively to speak loudly, clearly, and with expression. Students must also use their bodies effectively to stand in position, gesture with energy and expression, and enter and exit the performance space appropriately. As with any theatrical presentation, these components require rehearsal.

Switching Roles: From Head Playwright to Director

Because CBRT emphasizes spoken words and gestures, not staged action or **blocking**, teachers who have little or no theatrical training can function effectively as directors. When the final draft of a CBRT script is ready for reading and rehearsing, your role shifts from that of head playwright to director. To prepare your students to perform a script—whether that performance is for the class down the hall or for a citywide assembly—you function as their stage director. You lead them through the rehearsal process, coaching them dramatically.

> **Blocking:** The official theatrical term for the actors' stage movement (e.g., entering, sitting, crossing from one position another, exiting).

In many CBRT experiences, entire classes perform together, thereby eliminating distractions from students not involved in the scene being rehearsed. Everyone is involved. Everyone must listen for cues, speak individually or with others, and execute the agreed-upon gestures. As director, you perform a familiar supervisory role. All students face you, remain alert for cues, speak their individual and group lines, and start and stop when you instruct them to do so. CBRT rehearsals need not consume entire class periods. Once the script is complete, rehearsals can occur in short amounts of time (10–20 minutes) over several class periods, thereby eliminating the need to use whole class periods as practice sessions. Revisit the CBRT Instructional Schedule in Figure 2 on page 20 for an overview of the sequence and pacing of rehearsals and all of the components of CBRT.

Distributing Scripts and Assigning Permanent Roles

Distribute the final draft of the CBRT script to students and prepare to note which student speaks which part. Now you are ready for permanent line assignments. You may choose to give lines to a speaker who read the lines well in a read-through. You may honor students' requests for particular lines. Overwhelmingly, however, distribution of parts in CBRT is random—"Who wants to read number 1? Number 2? Number 20?" and so on. Students volunteer, receive a number, and the parts are rapidly distributed without time-consuming **auditions**.

> **Audition:** A try-out performance in which actors read or perform for a director in order to be considered for a role in a production.

Regardless of whether a student has a solo part, all students read the script and speak the lines designated as "All." Therefore, students need not be forced into reading solo. There's something motivating about a script, however, and it's amazing and gratifying how many struggling readers clamor for solo parts. In such cases, you may be aware that parts 12 and 14, for example, have just a few short lines and you may want to assign those numbers to less capable oral readers.

Other factors to bear in mind when assigning roles are speech impediments, dialects, and limited experience in speaking English. For example, try to avoid giving a student who lisps lines with numerous /s/ sounds. Consider whether a student's dialect will make certain words or phrases in a line incomprehensible. If so, you may choose to avoid assigning those lines to that student. However, you may instead want to use CBRT as an opportunity to work on pronunciation, particularly with difficult technical terms or vocabulary words that are part of the unit and may be challenging for any student to pronounce. Students with limited English proficiency can often handle short solo lines like "What?" or "Oh, no!" and do so proudly and enthusiastically.

Having Students Highlight Their Lines

With highlighting markers, students should highlight their scripts each time they speak or gesture. Remind them to highlight the entire line, not just their assigned speaking number, because that helps their eyes keep on track during reading. Also remind them to highlight all of the "All" lines.

This step in CBRT is always a favorite for students as they begin to take ownership of their roles. "Is this my line?" "If I am number 4, do I speak where it says 1–5?" "Oh! I say every line with 'All?'"

When they are done, ask students to read through their lines silently and ask for any pronunciation help they need. Emphasize also that they should become familiar with the line or gesture that comes before their lines. Those are their "cues," the words or gestures that signal their words or gestures.

Holding the Initial Read-Through, or "Stumble-Through"

Once the scripts are highlighted, it's time for the first read-through—or **stumble-through**—because even with professional actors, an early run-through of a script is rough at best.

As described in chapter 2, at the start of any theatrical rehearsal period, the cast assembles for a read-through of the script. This occasion does not call for any stage movement. All actors remain seated and read through the entire script, each actor following the lines of dialogue and reading the appropriate parts aloud. Actors often call initial rehearsals "stumble-throughs" because of the unpolished nature of the emerging performance. Students enjoy knowing this bit of theater jargon, and it seems to diminish anxiety when everyone expects the first reading of the script to be a "stumble-through." Readers will mispronounce words, miss cues, lose places, speak too softly, emphasize incorrectly, and skip words—and that's OK. The important thing is that all students be gentle and encouraging with one another because mistakes are anticipated in stumble-throughs.

So, with your students seated, hold the first oral reading. Just do it and get through it. The second and third times through will show remarkable improvement in oral fluency, vocal expression, and **cue pick-ups**. Your written CBRT script, like scripts in professional productions, may undergo more changes, but any adjustments should be minor ones that students can pencil in.

> **Stumble-Through:** An unpolished complete run-through of a play.

> **Cue Pick-Ups:** The precision with which the actor responds to cues and delivers lines in keeping with the established tempo of the performance piece.

Making Decisions About Gestures and Sound Effects

At this point, as the script is read aloud, you and the students will make decisions about gestures and sound effects. In CBRT, because students need to hold their scripts even in performance, remind them to create gestures that can be performed with the hand that is not holding the script. For a uniform performance look, all students should hold their scripts in the same hand and gesture with the remaining free hand. Most commonly, this means scripts in left hands, gestures with right hands. (Yes—for aesthetic purposes—even the left-handed students.)

Some gestures and sound effects are easily determined and agreed upon by the students. For example, consider the stage directions indicated in the following portion of a CBRT script on segregation. (See Appendix A, page 79, for the full script.)

9:	A bunch of white people got on, and the bus driver said	**11:**	and Rosa Parks
10:	"Y'all move to the back now and give these people your seats!"	**All:**	refused! [gesture] [sound effect]

The gesture accompanying "Refused!" would likely be a flat palm held out toward the audience. This sound effect might be an uttering of "Uh-unh" or "Hmph!" When you get to a *[sound effect]* or *[gesture]* stage direction in the script, ask the students for their ideas. As much as possible, solicit and use students' suggestions. Even if you think you have a better idea, seeking and using the students' creativity contributes greatly to their commitment to and enthusiasm for CBRT.

In the interest of time, because you are the director, you may choose the first viable idea for a gesture or a sound effect contributed by a student—"OK, it's a flat palm and 'Uh-unh.' Let's continue." With several viable suggestions, you may model each suggested gesture or sound effect while the students watch, and then ask for and proceed with their preference.

However the choices are made, it's best to decide quickly, set the gestures and sound effects, and refrain from changing them once they are set. It's difficult for students to "unlearn" rehearsed gestures and sound effects.

Encouraging Students to Mark Their Scripts for Emphasis

Depending on the needs of your students, you may want the exact gestures and sound effects—"thumbs up" or "groan" for example—to appear right on their written scripts. You may retype the script with the descriptive stage directions or have students pencil them in. In most cases, however, this specificity is unnecessary because repeated rehearsals of the words, gestures, and sound effects cause students to remember them.

Students may find it helpful to underline certain emphasized words or phrases on their scripts. They may also want to indicate pauses or write pronunciation guides. Encourage any script markings that help students to feel more confident and perform more effectively.

Soliciting and Using Student Ideas

One of the pleasures of collaborating with students on the writing, rehearsing, and performing of a CBRT script is that you do not have to solve all the dramatic problems and come up with all the creative ideas. Good stage directors rely on the creativity of their actors. Your students are your best resource. When you encounter a problematic situation—how to deliver a line reading in unison, how to make a section of the script more interesting or humorous, how long to pause, how to emphasize a particular point—present the problem to your students and solicit their ideas. In most cases, their solutions are more imaginative and effective than any that occur to you! Soliciting, listening to, honoring, and using students' ideas also increase their ownership of the CBRT project.

SCRIPT SECTION: LIGHT AND SOUND WAVES

1: We're here to tell you about The Wave!

All: [gesture—the stadium "wave"] [sound effect]

1: Not that kind of wave!

All: [sound effect—confusion]

1: Wave as in light and sound waves!

All: Ohhhhh. [gesture]

2: There are many different parts to a wave...

3: What kind of parts?

4: Duh! Haven't you heard?

2: There's amplitude!

3: Ampli—what?

All: Amplitude! [sound effect]

5: And you better improve your attitude, son!

3: Yes, sir!

5: Amplitude is the height of a wave from its midpoint.

All: Amplitude [sound effect]—the height of a wave from its midpoint.

3: Can you put that in my terms?

6: [whispers] I hate learning about these boring waves.

7: Shhhhh!

5: Amplitude indicates the amount of energy carried in the wave.

Conducting Rehearsals

Beginning rehearsals are conducted with students seated at their desks. These rehearsals need not consume entire class periods. You can read through the script two or three times and then proceed to another activity. You can save rehearsal for the last 10 minutes of class. The goal of initial rehearsals is familiarity with the script—students repeatedly read, hear, create, and become familiar with the lines and sound effects. They practice performing the gestures energetically and correctly on cue.

In your role as director, lead all rehearsals—even those in which students remain seated—by facing the rehearsing students. "Mirror" the set gestures as you rehearse the CBRT script—if students are holding scripts in their left hands and gesturing with their right, you use the opposite hands. It is easier for students (even high school students) to follow you when you are a mirror image of the actions they perform.

Run through the script several times each day. When it comes to rehearsing, some classes are more enthusiastic than others. Some groups remain motivated through six or seven read-throughs; others are bored after two or three. Gauge your students' interest level and strive to keep rehearsals focused and lively.

Practicing Cues as Well as Lines

As mentioned earlier, students need to become familiar with their cues. A cue is the line, gesture, or sound effect that comes before any lines performers speak (individually or with others) and any gestures they perform. Cues deserve rehearsal attention, so remind students to review their cues when they review their lines. You may want to use a "cue pick-up quiz" as a rehearsal warm-up activity: In random order, read or execute your CBRT script's cue lines, gestures, and sound effects. Pause for the performers to come in on cue with the correct lines or gestures. Repeat any script sections for which the cue pick-ups are weak.

Assigning Stage Positions for Performance

Your CBRT stage is wherever your students will perform their script for an audience—the front of your classroom, the perimeter of your classroom or that of another teacher, the school stage, steps or risers, and so on. Your stage influences the positions your performers will take during the final rehearsals and for performances.

If you plan to invite audiences into your classroom or to the school stage for performances, you may assign your students standing and seated stage positions. Students can sit in chairs or desks with other students standing behind them. Some students may be assigned stage positions seated on the floor. If necessary, do what stage directors do—use masking tape or painter's tape (its light adhesive makes it easy to remove) on the floor to mark performers' positions. If you want to experiment with staging that looks a bit more creative, arrange whatever furniture or items you have in the performance space—tables, stools, chairs, desks, boxes, benches—and assign students a permanent sitting or standing position on or around them. If you plan to travel to other classrooms to perform, your performers' stage positions may simply be standing positions in one large semicircle around the front and sides of the classroom. See Figure 11 for some simple stage-position floor plans.

Your primary goal in assigning stage positions is that each student is clearly visible to the audience. Aesthetic balance and a pleasing stage "picture" may also influence your choices, as will your knowledge of which students you do not want positioned adjacent to one another! Students do not need to be arranged in the order in which they speak, although it may be helpful for pairs or small groups who speak lines together to be near one another.

Wherever your final performance is to be given, it's important to rehearse students in that setting or a close approximation of that setting. It is often difficult

FIGURE 11. CBRT Performers' Stage Position Options

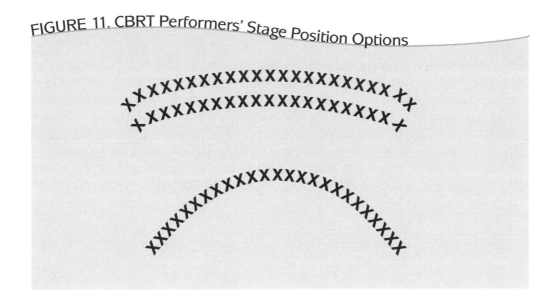

for young or inexperienced performers to rehearse in a classroom and then perform on a stage, in a hall, all-purpose room, or gymnasium. Familiarity with the performance space, the distance from the audience, the necessary vocal volume, and other factors all reduce performer anxiety and increase the quality of the presentation.

Coaching for Projection, Energy, and Expression

Anyone who speaks to a group of people has to speak loudly enough—project—to be heard and understood. Most students implicitly understand this need for a louder than conversational volume in performance. Some students, however, need coaching, coaxing, and support to "share their voices" without shouting. Assure them that their audience will enjoy energetic and expressive performances. Sometimes you need to coach them to be "bigger" in vocal and physical expression than they think they should be.

You may feel like a cheerleader at times, but it's often your modeling of vocal projection, expressive face and voice, and energetic execution of gestures that motivate students to give more than just a mediocre reading of the script. Give praise and show enthusiasm frequently during rehearsals. Laugh at the funny line deliveries and send silent signals of approval whenever warranted—thumbs up, nods, smiles, and cheering gestures. Remember that most students will mirror you, imitating the energy and expression you put into the script's words and gestures.

Sometimes, no matter how hard and long you coach, a student's solo voice will not be loud enough. One solution to this problem is to give the soft-spoken student the option of inviting a classmate to speak the lines with him or her. Most solo lines in CBRT work well with pairs of speakers, and enlisting the support of a peer is preferable to simply giving the student's lines to a stronger speaker.

Coaching for Speaking Lines and Performing Gestures in Unison

Rehearse and re-rehearse lines, gestures, and sound effects delivered in unison for timing and cohesiveness. All lines spoken in unison should receive the same line reading—the same inflections, tone, volume, and pace. Determine how performers will deliver all lines and sound effects performed in unison, and rehearse them for accurate group synchronization. The same applies to any gestures that the entire group performs together. Rehearse each gesture until all performers execute the same movements simultaneously with the same pace and energy. All of this speaking, sound effects, and gesturing in unison contribute to a more cohesive, pleasing performance.

Coaching for Concentration and Stage Presence

The acting skill of **concentration** requires performers to focus so well on what they are doing that they are not distracted by other performers or the audience. They keep their minds on their acting tasks and deliver a good performance. Concentration, especially with young performers, also means avoiding urges to giggle or crack up with laughter while rehearsing or performing.

Concentration: The actor's ability to remain focused on the acting task.

Introduce and discuss the need for concentration during rehearsals and performances with your students. Practice any humorous parts of the CBRT script to help make those parts more familiar and thus less laugh-inducing. Recommend that students practice focusing on the space just above the audience members' heads rather than looking at faces that could make them laugh. During rehearsals, challenge the CBRT cast to deliver the entire script without a single lapse in concentration. When students understand that concentration is an expectation and a criterion for success both in the theater and in CBRT, they overwhelmingly work hard to maintain it.

CBRT IN ACTION

The sixth graders and I had been working on the performance elements of their math CBRT script on Order of Operations. They had written a chant for the ending, and we were creating the gestures to perform during the chant. One girl was so good at remembering and executing the gestures, and I noticed that, as we rehearsed, she positioned herself slightly in front of all the other students. She clearly knew that she knew what to do and how to do it. One boy in that same class was also a definite leader in terms of performing both the gestures and the words. After class, I commented on these two students to their teacher who described them both as "always struggling" in her class. For CBRT purposes, however, I knew that I could rely on these two to remember and lead the other students during rehearsals and performances.

Explain to students that having stage presence means that they conduct themselves as prepared performers who remain calm, poised, and dignified whenever they can be seen by an audience. More understandable to students, perhaps, is what stage presence is not. It's not waving or signaling to audience members, rolling eyes, making faces, mouthing words, scratching itches, yawning, fidgeting, chatting with other performers, and so forth. State these nonexamples clearly (or role-play a student with poor stage presence), and you will likely elicit a few laughs. If you emphasize to students that their performance starts as soon as the audience can see them and does not end until they are out of the audience's sight and hearing, they learn an important theatrical principle and increase the quality of their CBRT performance.

Preparing Performers to Enter and Exit the Performance Space Appropriately

It's worth the time it takes to rehearse students in both entering and exiting the performance space. Toward the end of your CBRT rehearsal period, demonstrate how you wish students to enter the space in which they will be performing, find and take their stage position, await the cue to begin the performance, accept the audience's applause, and exit the performance space. After your demonstration, hold a rehearsal in which students practice entering and exiting appropriately with stage presence.

Troubleshooting—Preparing Performers for Possible Mistakes

It's rare that any performance will go perfectly, so prepare students ahead of time for possible mistakes and reassure them that this is normal and to be expected. The most common performance mistakes are missed cues and lines, **stepping on lines**, skipping lines, and reading lines incorrectly. Because students are holding scripts in CBRT performances, these mistakes are less common, but they should be addressed.

> **Stepping on Lines:** One actor beginning to speak before another actor finishes.

Emphasize to students that, as long as they do not show evidence of an error in their behavior (e.g., rolling eyes, grimacing, elbowing or scolding one another, saying "Oops"), the audience is unlikely to realize performance mistakes. Prepare students for the likelihood of errors and coach them to proceed as smoothly and calmly as possible. You can practically guarantee that if they do so, no audience member will be aware that the performance was less than perfect.

What if a student misses a cue and does not come in with a line? Remind students that everyone will be holding a copy of the script containing all lines. If someone does not come in with a line in a reasonable amount of time, anyone paying attention has permission to deliver that line. If several performers begin to deliver the missed line, that's perfectly acceptable and they should all keep on speaking together. The audience need never know, and the students who miss lines are encouraged to be grateful to their classmates for their teamwork.

Because CBRT is always performed with scripts, absent students are not a problem. Assign their lines to other students (**understudies**) who have heard them recited previously. They can read them from the script with little preparation, often delivering the lines precisely as the absent performers spoke them in previous readings. A quick adjustment and the performance proceeds as planned.

> **Understudy:** An actor who prepares to play a role in the place of an actor who must miss a performance.

Preparing for the Performance

The CBRT performance is also a product. It is a synthesis of knowledge and skills requiring students to make and carry out artistic decisions, use theatrical skills, and work together to present their CBRT script. The following section will help you and your students prepare for this performance product.

Outlining Performance Criteria and Providing an Assessment Checklist

What does a really strong CBRT performance look and sound like? How do high-quality CBRT performers behave while performing? What skills do they practice and exhibit? Why do performers strive to deliver strong performances? These questions are addressed in the list of assessment criteria provided in Figure 12. These criteria identify CBRT performance behaviors valued by theater and education professionals. Theatrically speaking, there are many performing skills that are identifiable and observable. These skills or behaviors are outlined specifically in this list to make students aware of the nature of excellence and what it takes to succeed when they perform CBRT (Arter & McTighe, 2001). To ensure that students understand these elements, review, discuss, and explain them in advance of any assessment.

These criteria are divided into four categories. The "Appearance" category concerns what the audience sees as the student performs. The "Vocal Qualities" category's emphasis is on the individual vocal aspects of the performance. The "Focus" category deals with the performer's concentration, attention, and poise while performing. The final category, "Ensemble Playing," refers to "the type of acting in which a cast works as a team to create a total effect rather than a group of individual performances" (Mobley, 1995, p. 49).

A more condensed version of this list of criteria is provided on the reproducible CBRT Performance Assessment Checklist on the next page. Each element in the left-hand column of the checklist identifies a desired performance behavior. To clarify performance goals, photocopy and distribute this checklist to students toward the start of rehearsals.

The structure of the CBRT Performance Assessment Checklist also allows for assessment of each element in varying degrees of proficiency with ratings of "consistently," "usually," "rarely," or "no evidence." The following descriptions explain each of these rating labels:

Consistently: The performer reliably and steadily exhibits the performance behavior described in this element in an accomplished, well-executed manner.

CBRT PERFORMANCE ASSESSMENT CHECKLIST

Performer's Name _____

The Performer...	Consistently 3	Usually 2	Rarely 1	No Evidence 0
APPEARANCE				
Enters the performance space appropriately.				
Holds the script correctly—in left hand, not blocking face/mouth.				
Exhibits good **posture**—weight evenly balanced; straight back; body remains still when not gesturing.				
Uses effective **facial expressions**.				
Performs **gestures** correctly and with energy.				
Exits the performance space appropriately.				
VOCAL QUALITIES				
Projects—has good vocal volume.				
Uses effective **vocal expression**.				
Articulates—speaks clearly.				
Uses an appropriate **rate of speech**—not too fast.				
FOCUS				
Maintains **concentration**.				
ENSEMBLE-PLAYING				
Works well in **ensemble**—behaves as a contributing member of the performance team.				

Total out of 36 _____

FIGURE 12. CBRT Performance Assessment Criteria

APPEARANCE

Enters the performance space appropriately.	The performer approaches the playing area or stage calmly with poise, composure, and self-control.
	The performer's facial expression and walk are self-assured and appropriately dignified for one about to perform for an audience.
Holds the script correctly—in left hand, not blocking face/mouth.	The performer holds the script at a reasonable reading distance—close enough to read, but not so close that the face and mouth are covered.
	The performer avoids rolling, flapping, crunching, or otherwise misusing the script.
Exhibits good posture— weight evenly balanced; straight back; body remains still when not gesturing.	The performer stands or sits in an upright position with weight evenly balanced. There is no slouching, sprawling, leaning, swaying, or fidgeting unless it is called for in the script.
Uses effective facial expressions.	The various looks on the performer's face accurately reflect the moods and sentiments of the spoken words and sound effects.
Performs gestures correctly and with energy.	The performer executes the rehearsed gestures with appropriate vigor, vitality, and intensity as opposed to merely going through the motions or gesturing in a listless manner.
Exits the performance space appropriately.	The performer leaves the playing area or stage calmly with poise, composure, and self-control.
	The performer's facial expression and walk are self-assured and remain appropriately dignified for as long as he or she can be seen by the audience.

VOCAL QUALITIES

Projects—has good vocal volume.	The performer's voice can be heard easily within the performance space. The performer speaks loudly enough but does not shout.
Uses effective vocal expression.	The performer's manner of speaking communicates the intended emotions, mood, or message of the written words or sound effects.
Articulates—speaks clearly.	Performers enunciate carefully so that their words can be understood. Performers pronounce distinct meaningful syllables and avoid slurring words and dropping the endings of words.
Uses an appropriate rate of speech—not too fast.	Performers speak slowly enough to be understood.

FOCUS

Maintains concentration.	The performer focuses on performance goals and avoids laughter, giggling, and distractions.
	The performer pays attention to and comes in on ("picks up") cues—any words or sounds that signal his or her lines, gestures, and sound effects.

(continued)

FIGURE 12. CBRT Performance Assessment Criteria (continued)

The performer exhibits stage presence, behaving with poise and dignity on stage. The performer avoids waving, making faces, rolling eyes, mouthing words, grimacing, and the like.

The performer remains focused during any mistakes that occur or covers for mistakes. The performer does not in any way signal to the audience that a mistake has occurred.

ENSEMBLE-PLAYING

Works well in ensemble—behaves as a contributing member of the performance team.

Because this is a group presentation, the performer works together with other performers as a team to create a unified performance.

The performer helps and supports other performers and the overall performance by

- performing group lines on cue and in unison.
- performing group sound effects on cue and in unison.
- performing group gestures on cue and in unison.

Usually: The performer largely exhibits the performance behavior described in this element, but there are occasional lapses in the steadiness and quality of the behavior.

Rarely: The performer only occasionally exhibits the performance behavior described in this element.

No Evidence: The behavior described in this element is completely absent during the performance.

The goal of the assessment checklist is to specify the performance behaviors that characterize an excellent CBRT presentation and provide a common vocabulary for discussing and working on its components. When students are aware of the elements that constitute excellent performance skills, they overwhelmingly deliver better performances. Like the CBRT Script Assessment Checklist presented in Chapter 4, this performance checklist was developed to help make CBRT assessment simple and informative. It also serves as further motivation for students to work on the specific elements that constitute the strong performances that lead to both increased self-esteem and greater learning.

Following the CBRT performance(s), you may use the checklist to provide your perspective on the quality of a student's performance. Students may use the checklist to assess their own performance and that of their peers. To convert the elements of the checklist into a numerical grade, use the suggested points assigned to each element category. Point allotments range from 3 for a determination of "consistently" to 0 for "no evidence." Adding up the points per element will result in a total performance score.

Anticipating Stage Fright

Even when they perform for just a small number of students in the classroom next door, many young performers feel nervous and their anxiety can affect their performances. This performance anxiety or **stage fright** bears discussion. Sometimes nervous energy results in better performances; sometimes students who were loud and dynamic in rehearsal are soft-spoken and reserved in performance. Talk with students about feeling nervous in front of an audience and ask them to share strategies for coping with stage fright.

Stage Fright: Anxiety before or during a performance in front of a live audience.

Arguably the best treatment for stage fright is repeated experience in performing. Work to instill confidence in your performers, praise them, reinforce your belief in their abilities, and send them back onto the stage.

Discussing Ensemble-Playing With Students

Be sure that students understand ensemble-playing as teamwork. Individual performers may deliver flawless performances, but the overall effect depends upon the united efforts of all students—the ensemble.

To encourage students to think about their CBRT ensemble performance, you may use the following questions in a class discussion about performing:

- What are the qualities of an effective ensemble performance?
- What do teamwork and an ensemble performance have in common?
- What should you as a group strive to achieve when performing?
- What should you seek to overcome when performing?

You may need to instruct and help students understand the importance of other performance skills that are necessary for ensemble-playing, such as uniformity of the **stage picture**. Establishing that CBRT scripts are held in the performer's left hand and that gestures are performed with the right hand is a simple way to achieve a uniform look for a CBRT performance. All performers hold their scripts in the same hand and gesture with the same hand. Uniformity of sound is another important element of ensemble-playing. All speaking and sound effects performed in unison should be delivered with the tempo, intonation, and expression practiced in rehearsals. In addition, it is necessary to exhibit uniformity of movement— all gestures performed in unison are delivered with the energy and movement choices practiced in rehearsals.

Stage Picture: The visual elements of the performance— what the audience sees.

The following questions can prompt students to consider other factors that contribute to successful performances:

- How do performers support one another in rehearsals?
- How does behavior in rehearsals affect performances?
- How do cooperation, attitudes, energy, and enthusiasm in rehearsals contribute to better performances?
- Why is it important to stick with the rehearsed ways of delivering lines, sound effects, and gestures in a performance rather than trying something new once you have an audience?

- How can lack of uniformity weaken a performance?
- How do performers support one another in performances? What if someone makes a mistake? How can others in the ensemble help? What should others not do?

After the CBRT performance has occurred, you and your students may reflect on it either to prepare for subsequent performances of the same CBRT script or as a culminating activity. If it is possible to videotape a performance, students can watch themselves and appraise their ensemble-playing.

SCRIPT SECTION: THE MAYAN CIVILIZATION

1:	Here today, in your school, we have Maya...	**7:**	what we know today as Central America.
All:	Ahhhhh! Maya! [gesture]	**All:**	Ohhhhh. Central America used to be Meso-America! [gesture]
2:	Oh my gosh!		
3:	Can I get her autograph?!	**8:**	Back then—AD 500 to AD 1500—
1:	Not the singer!	**9:**	Over five centuries ago?
All:	Awwww...[gesture]	**All:**	Duuuu-ude! [gesture]
4:	The civilization! [gesture]	**10:**	Meso-Americans just happened to be polytheists.
All:	What civilization? [gesture]		
5:	The Mayan civilization was part of Meso-America.	**All:**	What's a polytheist? [gesture]
		10:	A polytheist believes in many different gods.
All:	*Meso*? What does *meso* mean?		
6:	*Meso* means *middle*—		

Considering Additional Directorial Options

The additional directorial options outlined in this section are by no means mandatory. They are included here for teachers who wish to place greater emphasis on the CBRT performance.

Videotaping Rehearsals

Although many people remember to videotape a performance, few consider using videotape in rehearsals. It's a valuable tool. When students watch themselves on tape, they become acutely aware of deficits in their performances. Videotape allows them to witness performance problems—such as poor posture, scripts covering faces, weak gestures, inadequate projection, rapid speech, loss of concentration. It can aid tremendously in motivating students to improve in many performance skills. Positively speaking, videotape lets students enjoy and gain confidence in the strong aspects of their performance.

Adding Recorded Music

A CBRT project can be as simple or as elaborate as you choose. Recorded music played as an introduction or underscoring of a performer's words is an effective and mood-enhancing theatrical device. If you choose to incorporate recorded music, instrumental music, as opposed to vocal, is a wiser choice since a song's lyrics can overpower a student reader. You will also need to rehearse music cues, volume, and timing. For public performances, you may also need to research copyright issues.

Using Microphones

When a performance space is so large that hearing requires microphones, remember then that you must rehearse with microphones. Student performers are too inexperienced to adapt to speaking into a microphone without rehearsal. If the microphones are set up to capture sound from all directions, then no additional rehearsal should be necessary. If, however, students need to approach and speak into microphones, they need direction and practice.

Using Costumes or Props

You may certainly choose to use costumes and props in your CBRT performance, but they are not a necessity. If you do use them, it's best to keep them simple. Elaborate costumes, too many props, or props that are too complex may cause more problems than they are worth: Students forget to bring them and then feel they cannot do the performance; the props become damaged; students drop the props during the performance, causing the props to take all the performers' and audience's focus; and so on. Simple signs hung around students' necks, hats, large nametags, and the like, if they enhance the performance, can be used effectively. The best CBRT performances, however, require performers to rely primarily on their voices and gestures to communicate with their audiences.

Formatting, Organizing, and Preserving the Scripts

It's best to always photocopy or staple scripts back to back for smoother handling in performance. It's much easier to turn a page over than it is to flip to the second page of a stapled script. In addition, plastic page protectors are an excellent way to preserve scripts. They are strong and clear, maintaining scripts in good performance condition, and they live up to their name—they protect the pages!

Presenting CBRT for Selected Audiences

Whether it's for a schoolwide assembly in the auditorium, an evening parents' meeting in the all-purpose room, or the class down the hall, your students' CBRT

It's time for the sixth graders in an inner-city school to perform their CBRT scripts. The teachers and I have decided to end my arts residency by inviting parents as well as other classes to the performance that will occur on the school stage. We have rehearsed the students on the stage, which needs extensive clearing because it serves as the school's storage place. On the morning of the performance, I lead the students on one run-through of their script. They are antsy and squirmy, and I ask them why. "We're nervous," one of them tells me. I assure them that they know the script and they are ready to perform. "That's not the problem," they tell me. "We're nervous because we've never, ever been in a show on the school stage before."

performance is a significant part of the learning experience. The performance is what makes this reading and writing activity also an arts-integrated educational experience. It is the ultimate goal and motivator for all the previous work, but the students' learning does not stop at the performance.

Each performance experience allows students to reflect on what went well and to discuss mistakes and how to avoid them next time. There is nothing like an unsatisfying performance to inspire students to focus and rehearse more intently. Because CBRT performances are so integral to the students' learning, it's best to perform your script more than once. Arrange for your students to perform in several different classrooms rather than for one large audience of combined classes. Use the school stage, but invite classes to come to your CBRT performance one at a time. More performances mean more reading and more opportunities to improve reading fluency and performance skills.

Reflecting on the CBRT Performance

After your students' final performance of their CBRT script, allow some time for debriefing on the experience. Discuss what went well and what was positive about the individual and ensemble performances. Encourage students to compliment one another's work. Discuss what students learned about rehearsing and performing for an audience. Ask them what they would do differently if they had one more performance of the same script. Discuss goals for future performance work.

Use the CBRT Performance Assessment Checklist (see page 63) as an assessment tool for individual performance work. As stated previously, you may have students assess themselves, collaborate with you on their assessments, or you may provide students with your appraisal of their performance work. To determine whether students have met the content standards addressed by the CBRT activities, assess them as you typically would, for example, with tests, quizzes, or written or oral responses.

EPILOGUE

A recent reflection I recorded in one of my professional journals reads "I often wish I had a video camera behind me focused on the kids as we do the CBRT. I see their faces change as the session progresses. They go from lethargic, distant, flat affects to being amused, sparked, interested, motivated, engaged, animated, and finally *dramatic*!"

In these days of high-stakes testing, occurrences of the class play and opportunities for classroom dramatizations are diminishing. For many students, dramatic activities like Curriculum-Based Readers Theatre are their first and only chance to act in a performance of any kind. In a very small way, CBRT allows students to experience the feelings of excitement, anticipation, and nervousness that actors feel as opening night approaches. It involves them in the discipline of rehearsing something they fully created to share with an audience they hope to please. Participating as a member of a CBRT cast gives students a tiny taste of the power of a group of prepared performers who delight and impress their audience with movement, sound, and voices. Even if their stage is only the front of a classroom and their audience is only students seated at their desks, CBRT performers still relish the appreciation, laughter, and applause—all the while reading fluently and repeating the content information they are supposed to learn.

Sample Curriculum–Based Readers Theatre Scripts

THE BILL OF RIGHTS

Developed with students at Kenmore Middle School, Arlington, Virginia, USA

1: What is a right?

2: The correct answer!

3: Not being wrong!

4: Not on the left!

5: No—not those kinds of right!

1: Right—as in "It's my right to have fun!"

6: Oh, that kind of right—it's something you're entitled to,

7: something everyone deserves,

8: something you're allowed to do or have.

9: Like we're allowed to wear our own clothes to school.

All: Right! [gesture]

10: Like we can vote if we are 18 or older.

All: Right! [gesture]

11: OK, now that we've got that right, who knows what the founding fathers added to the Constitution?

2: The Declaration of Independence?

11: No! [sound effect—confused grumbling]

1: That came before the Constitution!

All: Oh yeah—the Bill of Rights! [gesture]

2: How much did it cost?

12: Not that kind of Bill!

3: Bill as in Clinton?

12: No!

3: Then what kind of Bill?

13: A Bill as in a law.

All: The Bill of Rights is the first 10 Amendments to the Constitution,

14: guaranteeing certain basic rights and liberties for all citizens.

15: Ratified in 1791, these 10 Amendments are...

16: The First Amendment...

17: We can follow our religion and not someone else's.

18: Cool.

19: Also, we have the freedom of speech.

20: What? Huh?

19: You can say what you want freely. [sound effect—all begin talking freely]

21: OK! [clears throat] And don't forget the freedom of the press.

22: You mean we can press all the buttons we want? [gesture]

All: No! The freedom of the press lets us print newspapers with our own thoughts and opinions.

23: Totally!

24: There's also the freedom of assembly.

25: You mean we have to go to a school assembly?

24: Kind of. It means we can meet together in groups freely.

All: The First Amendment—freedom of religion, speech, press, assembly.

1: The Second Amendment says that all states have the right to keep a militia.

2: Militia?

1: A defense, like an army, navy, or National Guard.

3: Also the Second Amendment protects the right of the people to bear arms.

4: Bare arms and wear tube tops! Yes!

3: Not the right to *wear* bare arms. The right to bear arms means the right to carry a weapon.

4: Oh.

Girls: The Third Amendment says that no soldier shall, in time of peace or war, be quartered in any house without the consent of the owner.

6: What the...?

5: Look here, it means that soldiers and troops should not live in people's houses without their permission. [gesture]

6: Isn't that just common sense? Why do they need to put that on paper?

7: Remember how the colonists were put under the Quartering Act?

8: When the British couldn't afford temporary housing?

6: Oh yeah—so the British made the colonists give their soldiers shelter.

8: Correct. So the founding fathers said our government doesn't have the right to do that.

7: Excellent. On to Amendment Four that states...

All: The right of the people to be secure in their persons, houses, papers, and effects against unreasonable searches and seizures...

9: [sound effect] Get on with it!

(continued)

10: What's it mean?

11: The colonists wanted the right to privacy.

12: People's houses and the people themselves cannot be searched without a warrant. [gesture]

10: A warrant?

13: A warranty?

12: A warrant—an order given by a judge. The police can't come in and search your house unless they have one.

13: I'll remember that. It's our right under the Fourth Amendment.

12: It also says...

11: Information or evidence of a crime that was found by searching a person's house without a search warrant cannot be used in court.

13: Next—the Fifth Amendment. That's a big one.

14: No person should be held for a crime without a grand jury.

15: What does that mean?

13: It means that all people have the right to a trial.

14: Nor shall any person be subject for the same offense to be twice put in jeopardy of life or limb.

All: Now we're really confused. [gesture]

14: It means that if you commit a crime and go to trial, you can't be tried again for the same crime.

All: Double Jeopardy!

11: Isn't that a movie?

16: Right—but there's another part of the Fifth here—nor shall a person be compelled in any criminal case to be a witness against himself.

All: Huh?

16: Say you commit a crime. When the police ask you, you don't have to tell them you did it.

All: We can claim the Fifth! [gesture]

15: That means we don't have to testify against ourselves in a court of law!

16: Right. And they need evidence to arrest you. They cannot arrest you just for looking suspicious.

All: Phew!

17: The Sixth Amendment—in all criminal prosecutions, the accused shall enjoy the right to a speedy and public trial....

All: OK, OK...translation please.

17: If you commit a crime and you get arrested, your trial must follow soon afterward.

All: ASAP! [gesture]

18: What if I don't have enough money to hire a lawyer?

17: The government has to give you one.

All: Got it. On to the Seventh Amendment.

18: The Seventh Amendment says that in suits of common law where the value in controversy shall exceed $20, the right of trial by jury shall be otherwise examined....

All: Say what? [gesture]

18: OK. It means that if you steal something worth more than $20, you have to go to federal court.

19: So if I stole something like a TV, I'd have a jury trial in federal court?

18: You could have a jury trial, but federal courts deal with the big money cases.

19: If I stole something cheap, like a can of soda, would you bail me out?

18: Probably not, but now that you've mentioned bail, that's the subject of the Eighth Amendment.

14: Excessive bail shall not be required nor excessive fines imposed

20: nor cruel and unusual punishments inflicted.

All: English again, please! [sound effect]

20: Officials can't charge too much for bail or fines.

21: So, like, if you stole a candy bar, they couldn't make your bail or fine $20,000.

22: And you couldn't be given the electric chair for stealing a TV either.

23: The Ninth Amendment says that "this enumeration in the Cons...."

All: [sound effect—groans]

23: OK, OK! If there are rights that they left out of the Constitution, the people still have those rights.

All: Your point is?

23: People have other rights that might not be in the Constitution?

25: Right. I guess they were afraid they might have forgotten some.

20: Good thinking. What comes next?

(continued)

25: The Tenth—the last one in the Bill of Rights, but there are 27 altogether.

All: Holy Cow! [gesture]

21: The Tenth Amendment protects the states and the people from powerful governments.

All: How?

21: Remember how King George was too controlling of the colonists?

22: He didn't give them any say in Parliament?

All: That's not fair. [gesture]

21: Right. So that's what the Tenth is all about—it says that any powers *not* given to the federal government...

All: Go to the states! [sound effect]

22: So the federal government doesn't get too powerful.

23: And those are the first 10 Amendments to our Constitution, which are called

All: the Bill of Rights.

24: I guess all Americans should know them.

25: Or people could take advantage of us.

All: Not us! [gesture]
WE [gesture] KNOW our rights!
Yeah! [gesture]

FRACTIONS

Developed with students at Douglass High School, Oklahoma City, Oklahoma, USA

1: Ladies and Gentlemen—I am pleased to introduce an improper fraction.

All: An improper fraction? [gesture]

1: Yes. An improper fraction has a numerator bigger than the denominator.

All: Hmmm. [gesture]

2: So the fraction five thirds—5 over 3—is an improper fraction?

1: Right.

2: So how do we make it proper?

3: Send it to manners school?

All: [groan]

1: No—all you do is see how many times the *denominator*,

4: the number below the line,

1: will go into the *numerator*,

5: the number above the line!

All: See how many times the *denominator*, the number below the line, will go into the *numerator*, the number above the line!

6: Like a division problem?

1: Yeah—fractions *are* division problems.

7: OK, so we see how many times the denominator 3 goes into the numerator 5

8: and write the remainder as a fraction...

9: and write the answer as a mixed number.

10: The answer is one and two fifths.

11: Oh! So a mixed number is a whole number with a fraction buddy by its side?

12: Yeah—you got it!

All: [gesture—high fives] [sound effect] A mixed number is a whole number with a fraction buddy by its side.

13: Hey—these fractions are sounding easier all the time!

14: What about adding fractions?

1: Well, first of all, the denominators have to be the same number.

All: [chant] For adding and subtracting, denominators—same, for adding and subtracting, denominators—same.

15: OK, OK—but what about fractions that don't have the same denominator?

1: Find the lowest common multiple between the two denominators.

All: The lowest what? [gesture]

1: Lowest common multiple—you know, count by the two denominator numbers until you find the smallest one on both lists.

16: So if we are adding two thirds—2 over 3—and three fourths—3 over 4, we'd...

All: count by the two denominator numbers until you found the smallest one on both lists.

17: Three—3, 6, 9, 12

18: Four—4, 8, 12

All: 12! [[gesture]

19: 12 is the lowest common multiple of denominators 3 and 4!

All: Score! [gesture] [sound effect]

20: So now what?

1: Change two thirds to eight twelfths—8 over 12—

2: and three fourths to nine twelfths—9 over 12—

3: and add them up.

All: [gesture] 8 plus 9 equals 17—the answer is seventeen twelfths!

4: Hey, isn't that where we started all this—with an improper fraction?

All: Uh! How rude! [gesture]

THE ONOMATOPOEIA FOREST

Developed with students at Kenmore Middle School, Arlington, Virginia, USA

1:	Once upon a time	**19:**	Well, that didn't work...
2:	in the Onomatopoeia Forest	**20:**	I know! How about a lot of lines of alliteration?
3:	a bunch of teenagers	**All:**	Yeah! Alliteration—words that begin with repeating consonant sounds.
4:	got lost!	**21:**	Running red rabbits
All:	[sound effect]	**22:**	grazed on green grass!
5:	Snap!	**23–26:**	Whoosh! Bam! Zap! Crack!
6:	Swish!	**All:**	[sound effect] [gesture]
7:	Splash!	**1:**	The onomatopoeia are still here....
All:	Uh! Oh no! What was that? [gesture]	**All:**	Aw, man! [gesture]
8:	That was the onomatopoeia!	**2:**	There must be some poetic device we can use to reverse the curse.
23–26:	Whoosh! Bam! Zap! Crack!	**All:**	Let's use rhyme with
All:	[sound effect] [gesture]	**3:**	alliteration
9:	Yes, this forest was cursed years ago to be filled with	**All:**	and
All:	words that imitate sounds—onomatopoeia!	**4:**	onomatopoeia!
10:	Tick-tock!	**5:**	Great idea! Let's write one now.
11:	Pop-pow!	**All:**	[gesture—thinking and writing] [sound effect]
12:	Clip-clop!	**6:**	I've got it! Repeat after me: Bash, bam, bleep, blare!
All:	Tick-tock! Pop-pow! Clip-clop!	**All:**	Bash, bam, bleep, blare!
13:	But that sounds like alliteration.	**6:**	To disperse this curse, that's our verse!
14:	You mean words that begin with repeating consonant sounds?	**All:**	To disperse this curse, that's our verse!
All:	Naw, ya think? [gesture]	**7:**	Is the onomatopoeia still there?
15:	Yes!	**All:**	[gesture] [silence]
16:	So what should we do?	**22:**	Finally! [gesture]
17:	To get rid of the curse?	**All:**	The curse is gone! [gesture]
18:	Let's try an onomatopoeia chant:	**5:**	To be continued....
14:	Screech, rattle, thud [stamp]		
All:	Outta the forest right now! [stamp twice]		
23–26:	Whoosh! Bam! Zap! Crack!		
All:	[sound effect] [gesture]		

SEGREGATION

Developed with students at Ben Davis High School, Indianapolis, Indiana, USA

1: Sorry, we don't serve your kind here.

2: Whites only!

3: You cannot use that drinking fountain!

4: But...

All: Sorry!

5–8: You can't go to our school.

9: Stop! Your restroom is down there.

10: Oh. Sorry.

11: What are you all talking about?

12: Don't you know that life used to be different for African Americans in the United States?

13: What do you mean?

14: How was it different?

15: Blacks and whites were segregated.

13, 14: Segregated?

All: Segregated. [sound effect]

4: Yes, they were separated.

All: Segregation is the social policy of separation according to race.

5: Whites had more rights? [gesture]

All: Right! [gesture]

6: Blacks and whites used different restaurants,

6, 7: drinking fountains,

6–8: schools,

6–9: and restrooms.

10: And even though they paid the same fare, blacks had to sit in

All: [sound effect] the back of the bus!

16: Man, why'd anybody put up with that?

All: Jim Crow! [gesture] [sound effect]

17: Who's Jim Crow?

18: Jim Crow is an insulting slang term for a black person.

All: The laws that permitted segregation were called Jim Crow laws.

19: Jim Crow laws denied blacks civil rights like sitting at the front of the bus.

13, 14: Civil rights? What are they?

All: Civil rights are the fundamental freedoms and privileges belonging to a country's citizens.

20: All citizens!

1: In the 1950s and 1960s, civil rights came to mean the movement to secure equal opportunity and treatment for members of minority groups.

2: Equal job opportunities,

3: equal pay,

4: equal schools.

5: And no more moving to

All: [sound effect] the back of the bus!

6: Ummm-hmmmm. [gesture] Thanks to

All: Rosa Parks! [gesture] [sound effect]

7: Who's Rosa Parks?

8: She's a black woman who was riding on a bus in Montgomery, Alabama, in 1955.

9: A bunch of white people got on, and the bus driver said,

10: "Y'all move to the back now and give these people your seats!"

11: and Rosa Parks

All: refused! [gesture] [sound effect]

12: She was even arrested for this.

13, 14: Arrested?

All: Arrested! [gesture] [sound effect]

15: And then what happened?

16: Word got out, and all of Montgomery began the famous bus boycott.

17: Black people refused to ride any bus anywhere if the bus segregation law was not changed.

18: It took over a year, but the boycott worked!

All: [sound effect]

19: And Rosa Parks is credited with initiating the modern Civil Rights movement.

20: Thanks to Rosa Parks and others...

1: we all have the right to use the same restaurants,

1–5: drinking fountains,

1–10: schools,

1–20: and restrooms.

2: And never again will blacks be forced to move to

All: [sound effect] the back of the bus!

3: And that, fellow citizens, was just the start of the

All: condemnation of segregation! [gesture] [sound effect]

ENERGY

Developed with students at Monocacy School, Frederick, Maryland, USA

1: Boy, am I tired!

11–25: Me, too! [gesture—yawn or stretch]

2–10: You all need some energy!

11–25: Energy! Right! What's energy?

2: Energy is what gives living things or machines their power [sound effect].

3: Just have something good to eat [sound effect]

4: and drink, [sound effect]

5: and you will get some energy!

11: So food is our fuel?

2–10: Right!

12: Well what about our machines? How do they get their energy?

6: I know one way—FOSSIL FUELS!

All: Fossil fuels?

6: Right! We burn coal, oil, and natural gas.

All: Fossil fuels—we burn coal, oil, and natural gas [sound effect].

15: Cool. What more do we need?

2: Lots more!

15: Why?

2: Well, fossil fuels are nonrenewable.

All: Nonrenewable?

2: That means that once they are used up, they will be gone forever.

All: [sound effect]

2: So we need alternative energy sources that are...

All: renewable! [gesture]

3: Right! Energy that can be used over and over.

4: It never runs out!

13: OK, so what's a renewable energy source?

7: I'll give you a hint. The biggest, brightest, warmest source of the earth's energy is...

All: THE SUN! [sound effect]

8: The sun! [sound effect] Gives us light and heat! [sound effect]

9: The sun! [sound effect] Warms our water causing rain [sound effect]

10: that falls back to earth and feeds rivers, lakes, and oceans.

14: The sun! [sound effect] Heats the surface of the earth and stirs up wind. [sound effect]

All: The sun! [sound effect] Source of light, heat, rain, and wind.

16: Renewable energy—water power! Hydropower! Water wheels!

17: Renewable energy—wind power! Windmills!

18: Renewable energy—solar power! Heat and light!

All: [chant] Water, wind, and sun for heat! They all renew! They all repeat!

19: So I guess we're all set then!

20: Not quite. How about synthetic fuels?

All: Synthetic? [gesture]

20: Synthetic—fuels made from other things.

1: Like what?

11: Coal, oil shale, and tar sands can be made into fuels for machines and buildings.

2: So when you think synthetic, think...

All: [chant] Coal, shale, and sand with tar may be changed to fuel your car! Coal, shale, and sand with tar may be changed to fuel your car!

3: But what about geothermal energy?

All: Geo—what?

3: *Geo*, meaning "of the earth"

4: and *thermal*, meaning "heat."

All: *Geothermal*—heat of the earth! [sound effect]

3: It's another energy source from the hot, molten rock deep inside the earth.

5: This natural heat is trapped within the earth.

6: If we drill down deep, we can use it to produce energy.

7: Hey everyone! Did you know that recycled garbage can also be used as an energy source?

All: Recycled garbage? [gesture]

7: Right! Recycled garbage and organic materials are called biomass.

All: Biomass contains stored energy from the sun.

8: We can burn biomass, produce energy,

9: and get rid of garbage!

10: So the future for alternative energy sources looks bright!

All: Right! [gesture]

11: But we still have to conserve the energy we have today...

12: and keep searching for and developing energy sources that are...

1–5: clean,

1–10: renewable,

1–18: inexpensive,

1–25: and dependable! [sound effect]

Dramatizing the Content With Curriculum-Based Readers Theatre, Grades 6–12 by Rosalind M. Flynn. © 2007 International Reading Association. May be copied for classroom use.

WOMEN'S SUFFRAGE

Developed with students at Douglass High School, Oklahoma City, Oklahoma, USA

Note. Males speak odd-numbered parts; females speak even-numbered parts.

1: The year is 1905.

2: The women in the United States are angry.

1: They are demanding suffrage.

3: Suffrage?

All: Suffrage—the right to vote.

2: The men in the United States are angry, too.

1: Let's listen in...

5: A woman's place is in the home taking care of the kids

7: and cleaning!

Males: Stay in the house! Don't come out! Stay in the house! Don't come out! [gesture]

4: Women are equal to men, and we want equal rights, too!

Females: Equal rights! Equal rights! [gesture]

6: We want to get jobs.

8: We do not want to be forced to stay home and raise kids.

9: Men are superior to women. Remember who was created first!

11: You came from my ribs!

Females: [sound effect—loud grumbling]

13: Girls, girls, girls—let us men take care of you.

15: Just head on home, and we'll do the voting for you.

12: We want our rights, and we will fight for them!

Females: We demand political equality! Political equality now! [gesture]

14: You've let the black men vote!

16: You've let illiterate immigrant men vote!

18: It's time that all races of American women be allowed to vote!

Females: Suffrage now! [gesture] Suffrage now! [gesture]

Males: Stay in the house! Don't come out! Stay in the house! Don't come out! [gesture]

17: Women are not smart enough to understand politics.

19: They are too emotional to choose the right political leaders!

21: No wife of mine will ever vote!

5: I wear the pants and cast the votes in this family, and that's that!

20: Women are people—not property!

22: We demand the right to govern ourselves!

4: We demand the right to choose our own representatives!

Females: Equal rights! Equal rights! [gesture]

1: It looks like things got pretty hostile back then.

2: That's right—women had to face a lot of opposition and sometimes even violence—

1: from the very people they had to convince to pass the constitutional Amendment to allow them to vote—

Females: men! [gesture]

Males: Ummm, hmmmm! [gesture]

3: So when did it finally happen?

2: Congress passed a women's suffrage constitutional amendment by a narrow margin in 1919.

1: It was ratified by the states in 1920.

5: See—we took care of you little ladies!

6: Why you surely did! Wouldn't you like a little dinner now?

Males: Absolutely! [gesture]

Females: Then pull out a cookbook and make it, boys! We've got better things to do!

CURRICULUM-BASED READERS THEATRE

By Rosalind M. Flynn

1: What is Readers Theatre?

2: Readers Theatre is a rehearsed

All: group presentation

3: of a script that is read aloud—

4: NOT memorized.

5: Performers hold their scripts throughout the performance.

6: Lines are distributed among

7: individuals,

8, 9: pairs,

6–10: small groups,

All: and the whole group.

9: Readers Theatre emphasizes spoken words,

10: not staged scenes.

1: So the performers don't move around the stage and enter and exit?

All: Right!

1: They just stand there and talk?

2: Well, no. To make the performance more interesting, they add gestures that mean things like

3: welcome [all wave],

4: good idea [all give "thumbs up"],

5: stop [all hold hand up with palm facing out],

6: I don't know [all scratch heads].

7: The performers also add sound effects to spice things up.

1: Such as?

8: Groans [all groan].

9: Sighs [all sigh].

10: Gasps [all gasp].

2: Wind [all create wind sound].

3: Falling rain [all slap thighs with palms].

4–7: Music also adds to the entertainment value of Readers Theatre.

4: For example, humming "London Bridge is Falling Down,"

All: [begin and continue humming "London Bridge" under the words of the speakers]

4: enlivens a script about Elizabethan England,

5: the Globe Theater,

6: and the dramatic works of William Shakespeare.

7: So then—what's Curriculum-Based Readers Theatre?

8: It's Readers Theatre that's based on curriculum content.

9: It's scripts about facts and ideas that students are supposed to know.

10: Curriculum-Based Readers Theatre involves students in

1: researching,

2: writing,

3: revising,

4: rehearsing,

5: repeating,

6: and performing a script meant to inform and entertain.

All: Curriculum-Based Readers Theatre—[a rhythmic chant]
A different, / creative, / dramatic teaching tool
To work with information students need to learn in school.

THEMES IN *OF MICE AND MEN* BY JOHN STEINBECK

Developed with students at Yorktown High School, Arlington, Virginia, USA

1: *Of Mice and Men* is a novel about what's really valuable in life.

2: Yeah, like money!

All: Money! [gesture] Ch-ching!

3: No, like friends and family.

4: Money makes the world go round

5: and you know it!

6: Take an example from the book: How Crooks was poor...

7: He had no money.

All: Awwwwww. [gesture]

8: More importantly, Crooks had no one who cared about him.

9: It's like George said—"Guys like us got no fambly.... They ain't got nobody in the world that gives...

All: a hoot in hell about 'em!" [gesture]

10: Yeah, but even with a friend like Lennie, George is miserable without money.

11: But he's less miserable than others.... Take Candy, for example.

12: Candy had money saved, but the thing that made him happy was his friendship with...

All: his old dog. [sound effect]

1: So *Of Mice and Men* is more a story about friendship.

Evens: Candy and his dog.

Odds: George and Lennie.

13: George loves Lennie.

14: What? No he doesn't! He killed Lennie.

All: He killed him out of love. [gesture]

14: So? He still took another man's life!

13: He was doing Lennie a favor.

14: Why would you think that?

13: Because those other men would have killed him if George didn't do it himself.

15: Plus—he let Lennie die happily thinking of his dream.

All: "...we get that little place an' live on the fatta the lan'." [sound effect]

16: If the other guys killed him, Lennie would have died scared.

17: It was like putting a dog to sleep.

All: Yeah! [gesture]

18: But what about all the times George yelled at Lennie?

19: And told him how much better his life would be without him?

20: He was just frustrated.

1: Besides, he had to put up with Lennie being clueless all the time.

2: Lennie was simple-minded,

7: but George is kind to Lennie...

8: because of his lack of intelligence.

9: And he never left him. He stuck by him.

All: Like good friends do. [gesture]

4: Well, I think George would have been much better off if he didn't have to deal with Lennie as a friend.

10: Well, you know what Crooks said—

All: "A guy needs somebody to be near him."

4: Yeah, but...

All: "He goes nuts if he ain't got nobody."

4: Yeah, but...

11: And Slim said—

All: "There's not many guys who travel around together."

4: I know, but...

All: "Maybe ever'body in the whole damn world is scared of each other."

4: But...

All: "Funny how you and him string along together."

4: But you still wouldn't shoot your friend, would you?!

All: [gesture] Hmmmmmm....

12: Lennie was just like Candy's poor dog.

13: He couldn't take care of himself.

14: He could no longer enjoy life.

15: Just like...

All: Lennie!

16: Lennie could not have enjoyed life, so George killed him.

17: He did it out of kindness.

18: He knew Lennie couldn't understand the consequences of his actions.

4: Because in order to love your friends...

All: you've got to do what's best for them. [gesture]

THE ORDER OF OPERATIONS

Written by students at C.H.A.T. Academy, Selma, Alabama, USA

All: What does 5 plus 2 times 3 equal?

1: [gesture] I got it! It's 21.

2: [gesture and sound effect] Wrong answer. It's 11.

All: But both answers could be right. How can that be? [gesture]

3: Our teacher told us that there could only be one correct answer.

All: How do we know which one is the right one?

4: Take a guess at it.

5: Do "eenie meanie minie mo"?

6: Pray really hard.

1: No, you don't have to do any of those. There is an easier way to do this. We will use a method called the order of operations.

All: The order of operations? What's that? [gesture]

2: The order of operations is a specific order for evaluating expressions so that we all get the same correct answer.

All: How do we do the order of operations?

3: We do the order of operations in the following magnificent way.

4: I am a grouping symbol.

All: What's a grouping symbol?

4: Grouping symbols are brackets, braces, and parentheses. You perform all operations within any of my symbols first.

5: I am an exponent. You evaluate all my powers next.

6: I am multiplication.

7: And I am division.

6, 7: Perform any of our operations next.

All: Going from left to right. [gesture]

8: [prop] I am addition.

9: [prop] And I am subtraction.

8, 9: We're next in the order of operations.

All: Going from left to right [gesture]

10: To sum it up, there is a chant we can use. All together now.... And a 1...and a 2...and a 1, 2, 3....

All: [chant]
Parentheses first!
Exponents next!
Multiplication and division in the same step! [gesture]
Addition and subtraction if you have the nerve—
From left to right, [gesture]
First come, first serve [gesture]

10: One more time!

All: [chant]
Parentheses first!
Exponents next!
Multiplication and division in the same step. [gesture]
Addition and subtraction if you have the nerve—
From left to right, [gesture]
First come, first serve! [gesture]

THE MIDDLE COLONIES

Developed with students at Wood Middle School, Rockville, Maryland, USA

1: Ladies and Gentlemen…[sound effect]

2: Introducing [sound effect]

1–5: Not the New England

6–10: Not the Southern

All: But…the Middle Colonies

3: Based on a chapter in YOUR Social Studies book

All: *The United States* [gesture]

1–5: *Its History*

6–10: *and Neighbors*

4: Written by

All: Us [gesture]

5: Starring

All: New York, New Jersey, Delaware, and Pennsylvania! [gesture]

6: also known as

6–10: "The Breadbasket Colonies"

7: Why?

Girls: [Rap] We're the breadbasket girls and we're here to say,
"Our colonies bake bread on every day.
Our fields yield crops of beautiful wheat
and other things most excellent to eat!"

8: What do you call a person who owned and ruled a Middle Colony?

9: A delegate?

All: No! A proprietor.

9: Then what's a delegate?

All: Delegates were people elected by colonists to represent them in colonial assemblies.

6, 7: Have you ever heard of Sarah Knight?

10: Isn't she the lady on *Good Morning America*?

All: [sound effect] [gesture]

6: No! She made a journey by horseback from Boston to New York City in 1704.

7: She wrote about how difficult it was to travel the rocky roads and cross the rivers.

1: When Sarah Knight visited New York, the Dutch influence was still strong.

2: What's *influence*?

All: *Influence* means the power of people or things to act on others.

2: Oh. Could you give me an example of Dutch influence?

3: Did you ever hear of a Dutch door?

2: Nope.

4: Well, it's a door with two parts. The top part could be open while the bottom part stays closed.

2: Cool.

8: Hey, I bet you don't know what pigs were used for in colonial cities!

10: Duh. They were used for pets.

8: Not. Pigs were used for cleaning up the garbage people threw in their gutters in the cities.

All: Yuck! [gesture]

HALLEY'S COMET

Developed with students at John F. Kennedy High School, Richmond, Virginia, USA

1: Attention everyone! The planets and their satellites are the most noticeable members of the sun's family.

All: Thanks for the news flash.

1: Let me finish. But there are many other objects in the solar system.

All: Like what? [gesture]

1: Have you ever heard of Halley's comet?

2: I have.

3: What is it?

2: Halley's comet is just a big dusty snowball.

4: Big deal.

1: Wait—what's in this big dusty snowball?

5: I know that answer. A comet has dust and rock particles mixed with frozen water.

6: And don't forget the methane and ammonia.

All: Methane and ammonia. [sound effect] [gesture]

7: How long has Halley's comet been around?

2: Since our grandparents were kids. [sound effect]

8: Longer. Since the dinosaurs.

9: When was the last time anyone saw it?

10: In 1986. It's only seen from Earth every 76 years. [sound effect] [gesture]

2: So we won't be able to see it again until...

All: 2062.

6: Man, our grandchildren will be digging our graves then!

All: [gesture] Maybe. Maybe not.

3: Hey, if we're still here the next time Halley's comet rolls around, I'll bring the chips.

4: And I'll bring the dip.

5: And we'll watch that dusty snowball from our comfortable wheelchairs!

All: 2062—be there! [gesture] [sound effect]

POLYGON NEWSCAST

By Rosalind M. Flynn

1: [TV news bulletin sound effect]

2: We interrupt this program to bring you an important news bulletin.

3: A two-dimensional figure was just spotted hovering over City Hall.

2, 3: Live footage from the scene.

4: Oh no! Not a polygon!

All: Oh yes! [gesture] A closed geometric shape with many sides!

5: Please, someone—tell us what you see!

6: Look, Mommy—there's a three-sided figure! [gesture]

7: Junior—don't look directly at it! It's a triangle!

All: [sound effect] It's a one- [gesture], it's a two- [gesture], it's a three- [gesture] sided polygon! A triangle!

8: Are all three sides straight? [gesture]

All: Straight! [gesture]

9: Are all three sides closed? [gesture]

All: Closed! [gesture]

10: Is the triangle on a plane?

11: No, it appears to be flying all by itself!

12: She didn't mean an airplane, dude!

All: In geometry, a plane is a flat surface. [gesture]

11: Right—plane...flat surface, man.

13: Look up again, everyone! [gesture] The triangle has some company.

14: It's a square!

15: It's a rectangle!

16: It's a rhombus!

17: It's a trapezoid!

18: It's a parallelogram!

All: It's the four-sided polygons [gesture]—squares, rectangles, rhombuses, trapezoids, and parallelograms!

19: Someone better alert the Pentagon!

All: Pentagon—a five-sided polygon.

20: Like the building in Washington, DC, they always talk about on the news?

All: Right! [gesture]

5: Who's got a cell phone?

All: I do. [gesture] [overlapping talking] Who knows the number? Can I text the Pentagon? Do they have caller ID?

11: I wonder why they didn't name it the Hexagon....

12: Duh—because the Pentagon has five sides and a hexagon has six sides.

6: Look, Mommy—there's an eight-sided figure! [gesture]

All: Eight-sided figure? An octagon? [sound effect]

7: Where's the octagon, Junior?

6: On top of that pole. It's red and it's telling me something!

All: [sound effect] What's it saying?

6: Stop! [gesture]

7: No, no, Junior! We need to know!

8: Ohhhh—he means the stop sign!

All: Oh right—a stop sign is an octagon.

6: It has eight sides and eight corners.

All: A corner of a polygon is called a vertex.

11: So, young man, your octagon has eight vertexes.

All: Not vertexes! Vertices! The plural of vertex is vertices!

9: Vertices—the points where the sides of the polygon meet.

10: Quiet everyone—she has the Pentagon on the phone right now!

All: [gesture—leaning in to listen]

13: What do they say about the polygons?

14: They say not to be alarmed. Polygons are harmless, and they're everywhere. Just look around you.

All: [sound effect] [gesture]

1: This is Polly Gonzalez with News Three-Plus signing off.

2, 3: We return you to your regularly scheduled program.

Curriculum-Based Readers Theatre Script Templates

The following CBRT script templates are tools that teachers and students can use to simplify the scriptwriting process. The templates offer a variety of contexts and provide sets of suggested opening lines and blanks for students to fill in with words or terms appropriate to the curriculum content of their CBRT script. Rather than creating a brand new CBRT script context, choose (or allow students to choose) from among the script templates provided and move more quickly into the scriptwriting.

CBRT Script Template—Television Competition

Note. This template is only a guide or a pattern to jumpstart your thinking. Feel free to make any changes in the words to better suit your original script.

CURRICULUM TOPICS: VOCABULARY OR TERMS

1: Ladies and gentlemen— _____

2: welcome to tonight's presentation of— _____

All: American Word Idol! [sound effect] _____
[gesture]
_____

3: Where words compete by sharing their _____
definitions!

4: Please welcome our first contestant, _____

_____. _____

All: [sound effect] _____

5: Good evening, I'm _____ _____

and my meaning is _____ _____

_____. _____

All: _____. _____

6: Next up is that challenging word— _____

_____. _____

All: [sound effect] _____

7: Yes, that's right. I'm _____

_____. _____

All: Hi, _____. Define yourself. _____
[gesture]

7: _____ _____

_____ _____

_____ _____

_____ _____

_____ _____

_____ _____

CBRT Script Template—News Report

Note. This template is only a guide or a pattern to jumpstart your thinking. Feel free to make any changes in the words to better suit your original script.

CURRICULUM TOPICS: HISTORICAL OR LITERARY EVENTS

1: Three, two, one, we're live!

All: [sound effect]

2: Channel Five Breaking News!

3: ____ years ago today, _____

4: _____

All: changed the course of history! [sound effect] [gesture]

5: This _____ was

All: _____.

6: Well, what happened?

CBRT Script Template—Tour Guide

Note. This template is only a guide or a pattern to jumpstart your thinking. Feel free to make any changes in the words to better suit your original script.

CURRICULUM TOPICS: GEOGRAPHY, SETTINGS, LOCATIONS

1: Good morning, travelers! _____

2: Thank you for booking a tour with _____

All: _____ Travel! [sound effect] _____

3: Where our motto is _____

All: _____. _____

4: Today's destination is _____

All: _____, _____

5: home of _____ _____

6: Yes, sit back and relax and get ready to _____

see _____, _____

7: _____, and _____

All: _____. _____

8: Hey, are we gonna see _____? _____

All: _____ _____

_____ _____

_____ _____

_____ _____

_____ _____

_____ _____

_____ _____

_____ _____

_____ _____

_____ _____

_____ _____

CBRT Script Template—Presentation

Note. This template is only a guide or a pattern to jumpstart your thinking. Feel free to make any changes in the words to better suit your original script.

CURRICULUM TOPIC: OPEN-ENDED

1:   Drum roll please! [sound effect] _____

2:   Sit back, [sound effect] [gesture] _____

3:   relax, [sound effect] [gesture] _____

4:   and most important—listen! [gesture] _____

5:   Yes! Today's fascinating (insert curriculum area) topic is... [sound effect] _____

_____

All: _____! _____

6–8: What's _____? _____

9:   _____ is _____

10:   _____. _____

6:   Ohhhhh! And that would be fascinating because... _____

_____

All: _____. _____

6–8: Ummm...a little help here.... _____

All: _____ _____

_____ _____

_____ _____

_____ _____

_____ _____

_____ _____

_____ _____

_____ _____

_____ _____

_____ _____

_____ _____

_____ _____

_____ _____

CBRT Script Template—Students in Conversation

Note. This template is only a guide or a pattern to jumpstart your thinking. Feel free to make any changes in the words to better suit your original script.

CURRICULUM TOPIC: STORY OR NOVEL

1–10: Guess what we just read!   _____

20: What? What did you read? I hope it's   _____
not another one of those
_____ books!   _____

11–13: Is it about an adventure? [sound   _____
effect—musical theme]   _____

14–16: Is it about a journey? [sound effect—   _____
musical theme]   _____

17–19: Is it about _____   _____

and _____ and...?   _____

21: Hey, hey, just let them tell what they   _____
read instead of guessing away all day!   _____

1–10: We read a story called...   _____

All: [sound effect]   _____

1–10: _____! [sound effect]   _____

22: Who or what is   _____

All: _____? [sound effect]   _____

_____   _____

_____   _____

_____   _____

_____   _____

_____   _____

_____   _____

_____   _____

_____   _____

_____   _____

_____   _____

CBRT Script Template—Students in Conversation

Note. This template is only a guide or a pattern to jumpstart your thinking. Feel free to make any changes in the words to better suit your original script.

CURRICULUM TOPIC: OPEN-ENDED

1: Hey—did anyone do last night's _____ homework?

All: Uh-huh.

1: Great. OK, what are _____?

All: _____!

1: C'mon you guys!

2: All right. Let's help him out. _____ are

_____

_____.

All: Oh—those _____! [sound effect]

3: Right—_____ is like

_____.

1: You mean _____?

All: Um-hmm! [gesture]

_____

_____

_____

_____

_____

_____

11: Gotta run.

12: Time for sixth period.

13: See ya after school.

14: Peace out.

1: Thanks for your help!

CBRT Script Template—Homework Hotline

Note. This template is only a guide or a pattern to jumpstart your thinking. Feel free to make any changes in the words to better suit your original script.

CURRICULUM TOPIC: OPEN-ENDED

1: [sound effect—ringing phone] _____

2: Hello. Welcome to the _____

All: Homework Hotline! [sound effect] _____

3: 1-800-H-O-M-E-W-O-R-K! _____

4: ...where students get lots of help with their _____

_____

All: hard homework! [sound effect] [gesture] _____

5: Press 1 for Math. _____

6: Press 2 for Social Studies. _____

7: Press 3 for Science. _____

8: [sound effect] _____

9: You have selected _____. _____

10: Please hold for your Homework Hotline Helpers! _____

_____

11: [sound effect] Homework Hotline! _____

8: Wuuuzzz up? I mean, Help! I need homework help! _____

_____

11: Go on. What's your problem? _____

5: _____ _____

_____ _____

_____ _____

_____ _____

_____ _____

_____ _____

_____ _____

CBRT Script Template—TV Show

Note. This template is only a guide or a pattern to jumpstart your thinking. Feel free to make any changes in the words to better suit your original script.

CURRICULUM TOPIC: OPEN-ENDED

1: And now for our program. _____

All: [music] _____

1: Today's show is... _____

All: "_____ _____

_____!" [gesture] _____

2: The TV show about _____

All: _____! [gesture] _____

3: Yes, we'll be talking about _____. _____

4: Let's start with _____. _____

All: [sound effect] _____

_____ _____

_____ _____

_____ _____

_____ _____

_____ _____

_____ _____

_____ _____

_____ _____

_____ _____

_____ _____

_____ _____

_____ _____

_____ _____

_____ _____

CBRT Script Template—Commercial

Note. This template is only a guide or a pattern to jumpstart your thinking. Feel free to make any changes in the words to better suit your original script.

CURRICULUM TOPIC: OPEN-ENDED

1: And now for a message from our sponsor— _____

_____

2: Are you _____? _____

3: Are you _____? _____

4: Are you _____? _____

1: Then, you need _____

All: _____! [sound effect] [gesture] _____

5: That's right! With _____, you will _____

All: _____. _____

6: Here's how it works: _____

_____   _____

_____   _____

_____   _____

_____   _____

_____   _____

_____   _____

_____   _____

_____   _____

_____   _____

_____   _____

_____   _____

_____   _____

_____   _____

CBRT Script Template—Classroom

Note. This template is only a guide or a pattern to jumpstart your thinking. Feel free to make any changes in the words to better suit your original script.

CURRICULUM TOPIC: OPEN-ENDED

1:   Good morning, class.   _____

All: Good morning, _____.   _____

1:   Welcome to the first day of school.   _____

All: [sound effect]   _____

1:   Please open your _____   _____
         books to page 12.
                                                                           _____

All: [sound effect]   _____

2:   Teacher, it's the first day of school!   _____

3:   It's too soon to start learning!   _____

All: [sound effect][gesture]   _____

1:   Boys and girls, it is never too soon to start   _____
         learning! Today's cool curriculum topic is
                                                                           _____
         _____.
                                                                           _____

All: Cool. [sound effect] [gesture]   _____

4:   OK, so what do we need to know?   _____

         _____   _____

         _____   _____

         _____   _____

         _____   _____

         _____   _____

         _____   _____

         _____   _____

         _____   _____

         _____   _____

CBRT Script Template—Newspaper Report

Note. This template is only a guide or a pattern to jumpstart your thinking. Feel free to make any changes in the words to better suit your original script.

CURRICULUM TOPIC: OPEN-ENDED

1: Extra! Extra! _____

2: Read all about it! _____

3: Get your copy of the _____ _____

_____ News right here! _____

4: In this issue—all the news that's fit to print about _____

_____

5: _____! _____

All: _____? _____
[sound effect][gesture]

5: That's what I said! _____

6: You'll read all the details of _____ _____

_____! _____

All: [sound effect] [gesture] _____

7: There are interviews with _____ _____

_____! _____

All: _____? [sound effect] [gesture] _____

7: Ummm, hmmm... _____

All: [gesture] [sound effect—scrambled voices—e.g., "I want a copy!" "One for me!"] _____

_____

8: Look what it says here: _____ _____

_____! _____

All: [sound effect] [gesture] _____

9: And then, _____! _____

_____ _____

_____ _____

_____ _____

CBRT Script Template—TV Quiz Show

Note. This template is only a guide or a pattern to jumpstart your thinking. Feel free to make any changes in the words to better suit your original script.

CURRICULUM TOPIC: OPEN-ENDED

1: Up next on Channel 444—

2: Stay tuned for everyone's favorite quiz show—

All: _____!

[sound effect—quiz show theme music]

3: Please welcome your hosts—_____
_____!

All: [sound effect] [gesture]

4: Thank you, fans. Thank you! Tonight, our contestants will compete for the jackpot prize of _____!

All: [sound effect]

5: So let's get the show rolling! All of tonight's quiz questions will be on the topic of

All: _____!

4: Contestant number 1—Your question:

_____

_____

6: Is it _____?

All: [sound effect] [gesture]

5: Oh, I'm sorry. That is incorrect. Contestant Number 2, do you know the answer?

7: _____

_____

_____

_____

Dramatizing the Content With Curriculum-Based Readers Theatre, Grades 6–12 by Rosalind M. Flynn. © 2007 International Reading Association. May be copied for classroom use.

Computer Formatting the Curriculum-Based Readers Theatre Script

1. Begin by typing the lines without indicating numbered speakers or "All."

   Who wants some candy?
   Me!
   But I only have one whole candy bar!
   Oh, man!
   I have to buy my own, then.
   Oh, snap!
   I know how you can share your whole bar! I know how you can share your whole bar!
   Great! How?
   You need to know about fractions.
   Fractions? What is a fraction?
   A fraction is a part of a whole.

2. Go back through the script and indicate speakers by numbers or "All" (or other descriptors). (You may need to turn off your word processing program's AutoFormat option, which automatically numbers lists as you type.)

   • Insert a Tab and a colon after the number or "All" and before the beginning of the speaker's line.

   • Insert [gesture] or [sound effect] where appropriate.

   1:   Who wants some candy?
   All: Me! [gesture]
   1:   But I only have one whole candy bar!
   All: Oh, man! [gesture]
   2:   I have to buy my own, then.
   3:   Oh, snap!
   4:   I know how you can share your whole bar! I know how you can share your whole bar!
   All: Great! How? [gesture]
   4:   You need to know about fractions.
   All: Fractions? What is a fraction? [gesture]
   5:   A fraction is a part of a whole.

3. Highlight all of the script's dialogue and format it to have a hanging indent. On some word-processing programs, this can be accomplished by pressing CTRL and T. On others, go to Format/Paragraph/Indentation/Special/Hanging. Using a hanging indent makes the script easier to read because the numbers for the speakers or "All" remain clearly visible on the left and the dialogue is easily distinguishable.

7: No! A whole is one entire thing—like a cake

All: or candy! [gesture]

8: See, your whole bar of candy can be divided into pieces,

9: sections,

10: or parts.

4: Those equal parts are fractions!

1: So, if I divide my whole candy bar into four pieces, and I give one piece away to Stacey, I still have three pieces left.

5: Right. I have a fraction of your whole candy bar. One of your four pieces.

All: Or one fourth!

4. Highlight all of the script's dialogue and format it to appear in two columns. On some word-processing programs, this can be accomplished by selecting Format/Columns/Two, and on others there is a toolbar option that can be used to indicate the number of columns, so you would need to select the option that shows two columns.

1: So, if I divide my whole candy bar into four pieces, and I give one piece away to Stacey, I still have three pieces left.

5: Right. I have a fraction of your whole candy bar. One of your four pieces.

All: Or one fourth!

1: And my three pieces are also a fraction?

2: Three out of four.

All: Three fourths!

1: Then, if I give another piece away to Derek, I have two pieces left.

6: My one piece is the fraction, one fourth.

1: And I still have two out of four pieces left.

7: Two fourths or

All: One half!

1: So if I give a third piece away to Maria, we each have

1–7: One fourth of a candy bar!

All: [sound effect]

5. You may need to experiment with sizes of margins (bottom, top, left, and right) and column widths and spaces, especially if you'd like the script to fit on one side of a page.

6. Regarding font size—generally speaking, the larger the font, the easier it is to read!

REFERENCES

Adams, W. (2003). *Institute book of Readers Theatre*. Chapel Hill, NC: Professional Press.

Alliance for Excellent Education. (2006). *Reading and writing in the academic content areas*. Washington, DC: Author. Retrieved July 30, 2006, from http://www.all4ed.org/publications/ReadingWritingAcadContent.pdf

Allington, R.L. (2006). Fluency: Still waiting after all these years. In S.J. Samuels & A.E. Farstrup (Eds.), *What research has to say about fluency instruction* (pp. 94–105). Newark, DE: International Reading Association.

Arter, J.A., & McTighe, J. (2001). *Scoring rubrics in the classroom: Using performance criteria for assessing and improving student performance*. Thousand Oaks, CA: Corwin.

Arts Education Partnership. (2005). *No subject left behind: A guide to arts education opportunities in the 2001 NCLB Act*. Retrieved July 26, 2006, from http://www.aep-arts.org/PDF%20Files/No SubjectLeftBehind2005.pdf

Badolato, S., & Domanska, M.A. (2002). *Implementing Readers Theatre: The benefits for teachers and students with learning disabilities*. Unpublished study, Chestnut Hill College, Philadelphia.

Biancarosa, G., & Snow, C. (2004). *Reading next: A vision for action and research in middle and high school literacy*. Washington, DC: Alliance for Excellent Education. Retrieved July 29, 2006, from http://www.all4ed.org/publications/ReadingNext/ReadingNext.pdf

Black, A., & Stave, A.M. (2007). *A comprehensive guide to Readers Theatre: Enhancing fluency and comprehension in middle school and beyond*. Newark, DE: International Reading Association.

Burnaford, G.E., Aprill, A., & Weiss, C. (Eds.). (2001). *Renaissance in the classroom: Arts integration and meaningful learning*. Mahwah, NJ: Erlbaum.

Catterall, J.S., Chapleau, R., & Iwanaga, J. (2000). Involvement in the arts and human development: General involvement and intensive involvement in music and theater arts. In E.B. Fiske (Ed.), *Champions of change: The impact of the arts on learning* (pp. 1–18). Washington, DC: Arts Education Partnership.

Consortium of National Arts Education Associations. (1994). *The national standards for arts education: What every young American should know and be able to do in the arts*. Reston, VA: Music Educators National Conference. Retrieved May 3, 2006, from http://www.menc.org/publication/books/natlstndartsedintro.html

Dixon, N., Davies, A., & Politano, C. (1996). *Learning with Readers Theatre: Building connections*. Winnepeg, MB: Peguis.

Fiske, E.B. (Ed.). (2000). *Champions of change: The impact of the arts on learning*. Washington, DC: Arts Education Partnership.

Flynn, R.M. (2004/2005). Curriculum-Based Readers Theatre: Setting the stage for reading and retention. *The Reading Teacher, 58*, 360–365. Retrieved July 25, 2006, from http://www.reading.org/publications/journals/rt/v58/i4/abstracts/RT-58-4-Flynn.html

Fountas, I.C., & Pinnell, G.S. (2001). *Guiding readers and writers, grades 3–6: Teaching comprehension, genre, and content literacy*. Portsmouth, NH: Heinemann.

Fowler, C. (1996). *Strong arts, strong schools: The promising potential and shortsighted disregard of the arts in American schooling*. New York: Oxford University Press.

Fredericks, A.D. (2001). *Readers Theatre for American history*. Englewood, CO: Teacher Ideas.

Georges, C. (2005a). *Efficient science instruction resulting from Readers Theatre integration*. Unpublished manuscript.

Georges, C. (2005b). *The lasting effect of Readers Theatre integration on oral reading fluency*. Unpublished manuscript.

Grumet, M. (2004). No one learns alone. In N. Rabkin & R. Redmond (Eds.), *Putting the arts in the picture: Reframing education in the 21st century* (pp. 49–80). Chicago: Columbia College Chicago.

Gustafson, C. (2002). *Acting out: Readers Theatre across the curriculum (literature and reading motivation)*. Worthington, OH: Linworth.

Harmon, S.D., Riney-Kehrberg, P., & Westbury, S. (1999). Readers Theatre as a history teaching tool. *The History Teacher, 32*, 525–545.

International Reading Association (IRA) & National Council of Teachers of English (NCTE). (1996). *Standards for the English language arts*. Newark, DE; Urbana, IL: Authors.

Jensen, E. (1998). *Teaching with the brain in mind*. Alexandria, VA: Association for Supervision and Curriculum Development.

Kennedy Center Partners in Education Professional Development Project. (2006). *Kennedy Center Partners in Education Professional Development Project*. Unpublished final report.

Kozub, R. (2000, May). Reader's theater and its affect [sic] on oral language fluency. *Reading Online*. Retrieved July 25, 2006, from http://www.readingonline.org/editorial/edit_index.asp?HREF=august2000/rkrt.htm

Larkin, B.R. (2001). "Can we act it out?" *The Reading Teacher, 54*, 478–481.

Martinez, M., Roser, N.L., & Strecker, S. (1998). "I never thought I could be a star": A Readers Theatre ticket to fluency. *The Reading Teacher, 52*, 326–334.

McMaster, J.C. (1998). "Doing" literature: Using drama to build literacy classrooms: The segue for a few struggling readers. *The Reading Teacher, 51*, 574–584.

Mobley, J.P. (1995). *NTC's dictionary of theatre and drama terms*. Lincolnwood, IL: National Textbook Company Publishing Group.

National Center for History in the Schools. (1996). *History Standards for Grades 5–12 United States*. Los Angeles, CA: Author. Retrieved December 15, 2006, from http://nchs.ucla.edu/standards/era3-5-12.html

National Research Council, National Committee on Science Education Standards and Assessment. (1996). Science content standards: 9–12. In *National Science Education Standards*. Washington, DC: National Academy Press. Retrieved July 26, 2006, from http://newton.nap.edu/html/nses/6e.html

Pikulski, J.J. (2006). Fluency: A developmental and language perspective. In S.J. Samuels & A.E. Farstrup (Eds.), *What research has to say about fluency instruction* (pp. 70–93). Newark, DE: International Reading Association.

Podlozny, A. (2001). Strengthening verbal skills through the use of classroom drama: A clear link. A summary of a meta-analytic study. In E. Winner & L. Hetland (Eds.), *Beyond the soundbite: Arts education and academic outcomes* (pp. 99–107). Los Angeles: The Getty Center.

Prescott, J.O. (2003). The power of Readers Theater. *Instructor, 112*, 22–26.

Rabkin, N. (2004). Learning and the arts. In N. Rabkin & R. Redmond (Eds.), *Putting the arts in the picture: Reframing education in the 21st century* (pp. 5–15). Chicago: Columbia College Chicago.

Rabkin, N., & Redmond, R. (2004). *Putting the arts in the picture: Reframing education in the 21st century*. Chicago: Columbia College Chicago.

Rasinski, T.V. (2000). Speed does matter in reading. *The Reading Teacher, 54*, 146–151.

Rasinski, T.V. (2001). Effects of repeated reading and listening-while-reading on reading fluency. *Journal of Educational Research, 83*(3), 147–150.

Rasinski, T.V. (2006). A brief history of reading fluency. In S.J. Samuels & A.E. Farstrup (Eds.), *What research has to say about fluency instruction* (pp. 4–23). Newark, DE: International Reading Association.

Ratliff, G.L. (1999). *Introduction to Readers Theatre: A guide to classroom performance*. Colorado Springs, CO: Meriwether.

Samuels, S.J. (1997). The method of repeated readings. *The Reading Teacher*, 50, 376–381. (Original work published 1979)

Samuels, S.J. (2006). Toward a model of reading fluency. In S.J. Samuels & A.E. Farstrup (Eds.), *What research has to say about fluency instruction* (pp. 24–46). Newark, DE: International Reading Association.

Schneider, D. (2005, March). Bearing witness through Reader's Theatre. *Book Links*, 54–57.

Scraper, K. (2005, May). *A dozen read-throughs and still going strong: Fluency and content knowledge via Reader's Theater*. Paper presented at International Reading Association, San Antonio, TX. Retrieved December 15, 2006, from http://www.edwriter.com/downloads/2005_ IRA_Handout.pdf

Sebesta, S. (n.d.). *The art of teaching: Readers Theatre*. Retrieved July 24, 2006, from http://www. teachervision.fen.com/literature/drama/6526.html

Shepard, A. (1993). *Stories on stage: Children's plays for Reader's Theater (or Readers Theatre)*. New York: H.W. Wilson.

Sloyer, S. (2003). *From the page to the stage: The educator's complete guide to Readers Theatre*. Westport, CT: Teacher Ideas Press.

Stahl, S.A., & Kuhn, M.R. (2002). Making it sound like language: Developing fluency. *The Reading Teacher*, 55, 582–584.

Stevenson, L.M., & Deasy, R. (2005). *Third space: When learning matters*. Washington, DC: Arts Education Partnership.

Tomlinson, C.A. (2001). How to differentiate instruction in mixed-ability classrooms. Alexandria, VA: Association for Supervision and Curriculum Development.

Trainin, G., & Andrzejczak, N. (2006). "Readers Theater: A viable reading strategy?" Lincoln, NE: The University of Nebraska College of Education and Human Science. Retrieved December 17, 2006, from http://digitalcommons.unl.edu/cgi/viewcontent.cgi?article=1007& context=cehsgpirw

Tyler, B.J., & Chard, D.J. (2000). Using Readers Theatre to foster fluency in struggling readers: A twist on the repeated reading strategy. *Reading & Writing Quarterly: Overcoming Learning Difficulties*, 16, 163–168.

Walker, L. (1996). *Readers Theatre in the middle school and junior high classroom*. Colorado Springs, CO: Meriwether.

Weinstein, C.F., & Mayer, R.F. (1986). The teaching of learning strategies. In M.C. Wittrock (Ed.), *Handbook of research on teaching* (pp. 315–327). New York: Macmillan.

Weissman, D. (2004). You can't get much better than that. In N. Rabkin & R. Redmond (Eds.), *Putting the arts in the picture: Reframing education in the 21st century* (pp. 17–48). Chicago: Columbia College Chicago.

Wolf, S.A. (1993). What's in a name? Labels and literacy in Readers Theatre. *The Reading Teacher*, 46, 540–545.

Worthy, J., & Prater, K. (2002). "I thought about it all night": Readers Theatre for reading fluency and motivation. *The Reading Teacher*, 56, 294–297.

LITERATURE CITED

Hawthorne, N. (2002). *The scarlet letter*. New York: Penguin.

Heaney, S. (2001). *Beowulf*. New York: Norton.

Irving, W. (2000). *Rip Van Winkle*. New York: SeaStar.

Juster, N. (1989). *The phantom tollbooth*. New York: Random House.

Konigsburg, E.L. (1996). *The view from Saturday*. New York: Atheneum.

Lawrence, J. (1995). *The great migration: An American story*. New York: HarperTrophy.

Lee, H. (2002). *To kill a mockingbird*. New York: HarperCollins.

Lowry, L. (1998). *Number the stars*. New York: Laurel Leaf.

Sachar, L. (1998). *Holes*. New York: Farrar, Straus and Giroux.

Steinbeck, J. (1993). *Of mice and men*. New York: Penguin.

Turner, A. (1997). *Katie's trunk*. New York: Aladdin.

INDEX

Note. Page numbers followed by *f* or *b* indicate figures or boxes, respectively.

Also by Rosalind M. Flynn

A Dramatic Approach to Reading Comprehension: Strategies and Activities for Classroom Teachers

Rosalind and co author Lenore Blank Kelner designed this book on four drama strategies—Story Dramatization, Character Interviews, Tableau, and Human Slide Shows—for teachers with limited experience in drama. Readers will find detailed explanations of how to lead effective educational drama experiences that increase reading comprehension.

Visit Rosalind's web site for information about her books and the professional development courses, workshops, and summer institutes that she presents.

www.rosalindflynn.com

Rosalind also offers online presentations about her Curriculum-Based Readers Theatre work. Complete information can be found at this web site.

www.ArtsEducationOnline.org

Read about Rosalind's work on her blog:

www.dramaticapproachestoteaching.com

DATE DUE

PRINTED IN U.S.A.

Made in the USA
Charleston, SC
07 October 2012